STRUGGLES:

Stories of Body, Mind, and Spirit in a Broken World

Bilbo Books Publishing www.BilboBooks.com
bilbobookspublishing@gmail.com

ISBN- 978-0-9981627-9-9
ISBN- 0-9981627-9-5

Printed in the United States of America
All rights reserved. Published in the United States of America by
Bilbo Books Publishing. Athens, Georgia

This is a work of fiction. Names, characters, businesses, places, events, locales, and incidents are either the products of the author's imagination or used in a fictitious manner. Any resemblance to actual persons, living or dead, or actual events is purely coincidental.

Photo Credits
Cover – from a photo purchased by the author from an unknown street vendor on the Charles Bridge in Prague, Czech Republic

Page 68 - Chattahoochee River, Columbus, Georgia, photo by the author

Page 71 – Old Man, from a photo purchased by the author from an unknown vendor in an outdoor flea market in Yerevan, Armenia

Page 80 – Ovens, Wiki. Creative Commons License

Page 87 – Man on Bridge, purchased by the author from an unknown street vendor on the Charles Bridge in Prague, Czech Republic

Page 123 – Alley from a photo by the author

Page 185 – Teary Eye, from a photo by Jan Saudek

Page 203 – Soldiers from the Everett Collection

Table of Contents

Dedication

Whether their problems are physical or emotional, real or imagined, billions of people struggle to survive every day. This book is dedicated to them.

Foreword

When my editor first read the stories in this book she described them, in part, as "borderline erotica." That had not occurred to me. However, sex *is* a common theme in the stories. Sex can be wonderful, greatly enhancing healthy relationships and marriages. Sex can also result in great shame, regret, guilt, and emotional pain. It can strengthen human bonds, and it can destroy them.

Each of my stories addresses one or more serious social issues, which are often couched in erotica. It is my intent in this book to encourage the reader to think about the serious social issues presented.

Crossing the River

Another Day

"ONE-OH-THREE...ONE-OH-THREE," THE RADIO CRACKLED. Then, a little louder, "Headquarters to one-oh-three." He roused from a light sleep he hadn't wanted but couldn't prevent, cleared his throat, and replied, "One-oh-three go ahead."

"One-one-eight Benning Road, see the party," the dispatcher ordered.

"One-oh-three clear," he responded. The dispatcher had saved him from falling into a deeper sleep, and from the nightmare.

Billy Ray arrived at the dispatched address five minutes later, at three o'clock in the morning. "One-oh-three, ten-ninety-seven," he said into the radio, giving the code for arrival and parking one house past his destination to avoid the possibility of being shot from inside the complainant's house. He exited the patrol car, surveying the house and the front yard, seeing and hearing nothing. The house was dark, no lights inside or out; with no streetlight nearby, the screened front porch was black.

He put his Maglite in his left hand in case he needed to get quickly to the gun on his right hip. He approached the house. It was *too* quiet. He reached for the screen door. "Stop right there!" said a woman's voice, softly but sternly. He froze, put his gun hand on his weapon, and shined his light in the direction of the voice. He could see that the woman was alone in the shadows. "Turn off that light!" she hissed, frightened. He did, and the woman said, "There's somebody in my house." He asked if she had seen someone; she replied that she had *heard* someone. She was adamant that he not turn on the lights in the house. He told her to remain by the front door, then entered the house, using his flashlight to check all of the rooms, windows and the back door, but he found nothing unusual. He turned on the lights and told her the house was clear. She asked whether he had looked in the bathroom. He replied that he had. She then asked whether he had looked behind the shower curtain, and he had to admit that he had not. He returned to the bathroom with the woman quietly following. He pulled aside the shower curtain. Nothing.

"Okay, ma'am, your house is safe."

"Did you look in the commode?"

Now he thought the woman must be a ten-seventy-four, a mental case. He nonchalantly leaned forward and raised the toilet seat on the largest sewer rat he had ever seen, standing on its hind legs not two feet from his face and shrieking an ear-piercing *eek! eek!* as it showed its long, dingy teeth. He stumbled backwards, slipping on a piece of toilet paper on the floor and falling on his ass. There was a loud bang—a gunshot! He looked up from the bathroom floor to see the woman waving a gun wildly above her head, shouting "Jesus! Jesus! Jesus!"

"Christ, lady, put the gun down!" he hollered as the woman continued hailing her savior. She ran to her bedroom and slammed the door. As he gathered his wits, he saw that the rat was now staring at him inquisitively from the toilet bowl, as if to ask, "What the hell are you doing on the floor?"

After fashioning a noose with a piece of rope, he removed the rat from the house, consoled the woman, and was happy to go "ten-eight," in service. He had heard it said that police work is ninety percent boredom and ten percent chaos. Boredom and chaos did account for some of a cop's time, but he had concluded that the largest percentage was simply bullshit, like this rat call. The rest of the morning was uneventful, and at end-of-watch he transferred the patrol car to his relief officer, turned in his portable radio, logged in his written reports, and went home.

Home was a cheap, one-bedroom apartment, sparsely furnished with second-hand pieces. He had been married and had had a home, but now he was alone. The Jehovah's Witnesses had knocked on the door and spoken with his wife. A year later she and his children were gone. He didn't blame her. He had loved her, but what did he know of love? The Witnesses offered her a passion that was missing in their marriage—missing in him—and had offered her a direction when he had none.

He may not have understood love, but he understood loss. After his ex moved with the kids to another city, he saw his children every weekend he could and cried on the ones he couldn't. He had seen suicides on the job and had twice drawn his weapon on suspects he later learned had hoped for "suicide-by-cop." He had concluded, rightly or wrongly, that there was a difference between being suicidal and having a death wish. As he saw it, putting a gun to your head was a suicidal act, whereas thinking sometimes that death would be less painful than life was something less serious, a death wish. He never put a gun to his head. But there had been a time, when he was first separated from his children, that he engaged in reckless, risky behavior. He would walk into bars cops never entered alone, just walk through the bar, his back unprotected, staring down dangerous men. Was that a death wish? Could it have been attempted "suicide-by-scumbag"? It was dangerous, but it was also exhilarating. Perhaps, he considered, the fear of losing one's life could cause one to fight to hold on to it. Billy Ray was a cop fighting to live.

The Golden Age

She was Billy Ray *and* Bobby's first love…and it *was* love. The kind of love that excites yet frightens a little. She was all they could think about during the school day, waiting for the last bell to ring so they could see her, be near her. She would take them both into her warm wetness. They were twelve years old, and *she* was the Chattahoochee River, which separated their sleepy Georgia town from equally sleepy Alabama.

The boys had been friends almost their entire lives, having lived in the same neighborhood, met in kindergarten, and graduated from high school together. Billy Ray's father had been a minister; and Bobby's family had been faithful members of his church. He and Bobby shared fond memories of Sunday school, Vacation Bible School in the summers, and singing in the choir. For the most part, they had both been blessed with good parents and "all-American" childhoods. Billy Ray's father had served in the army in Europe, and Bobby's in the Marines in the Pacific. Both men had come home to post-war jobs in the city's cotton mills. The boys didn't know what their fathers had done in the war because the men never talked about it. There were scars on Bobby's father's back, but when Bobby asked about them, his father would say only, "Jap bayonet." Eventually, Billy Ray's father was able to support his family as a full-time minister, and Bobby's father went to work for the city's public works department.

One of the boys' favorite games was to gather the other boys in the neighborhood, don surplus army helmets, belts, and canteens, and play war in "the woods," an undeveloped area just a block from their homes, which alternated as the scene of the Battle of the Bulge or Iwo Jima. They would play until dinner or even after dark, until the voices of mothers could be heard up and down the street calling the children home to their small mill houses for supper or bed.

At first, the boys' world was small. It was a four block walk to school, church, the grocery store, and the city park where they played little league baseball. Saturday baseball games were the highlight of the week. Their fathers had taught them the game and would play catch daily during the season. Billy Ray's father was encouraging and supportive. Bobby was the better athlete, but his father was more demanding and critical, always pushing Bobby to do better, play harder, to "be a man."

The boys' world had widened greatly when, at age twelve, they were allowed to walk the mile to the Chattahoochee by themselves to go fishing. Of course, they had been fishing since they were big enough to hold poles, their fathers baiting their hooks for them. Fishing with his father was one of Billy Ray's fondest memories, and his father would often preach of "crossing the river" as a metaphor for ascending into heaven. After Saturday morning baseball games, or after church and Sunday dinner, the boys would spend the day reclined on the river bank, hands behind their heads, soaking in the summer sun. They propped up their fishing poles with rocks, sometimes watching their corks for bites, not really caring whether the fish bit. One day as they lazed there, small waves from a passing fishing boat lapping against the sand and rocks, Billy Ray broke the long silence.

"I saw in a book in the liberry that the human body is 'bout 90 percent water."

"Uh huh," Bobby grunted drowsily.

"Our drinkin' water comes from the river. That means that ninety percent of us came from her," Billy Ray continued, poking Bobby's arm. "She's inside us. No, she *is* us, and we are her," he pronounced.

Bobby opened his sleepy eyes, squinting in the bright sunlight, and turned to look at Billy Ray. "You weird."

"Ain't weird!"

"Weird!"

"Ain't!"

The End of Innocence

Televisions had appeared in the boys' homes when they were ten. Billy Ray's dad referred to it as "the stupid box," but the boys loved TV. Daniel Boone and Davey Crockett killed the marauding Indians; Roy Rogers and Gene Autry killed the stupid bad guys in the black hats. (You knew the bad guys were stupid because they always wore black hats, which is how the good guys knew they were bad guys.). They watched Captain Kangaroo, The Little Rascals, Andy Griffith, and Leave it to Beaver. One day, Billy Ray realized he couldn't keep his eyes off those pointed breasts beneath Mrs. Cleaver's tight sweaters. Then he found that when looking at those breasts he wanted to touch himself, and *boy-oh-boy* (as the Beaver would say) did that feel good!

Bobby—athletic, handsome, and seemingly self-assured—found it easy to talk to girls, who all loved him. He was the envy of most boys in the school, including his best friend. Billy Ray was average-looking and shy with girls, but he couldn't keep his eyes off them or his erections in abeyance. His need for sexual relief was at times unbearable, and he quickly graduated from the women's underwear section of the Sears Roebuck catalog to old *Playboy* magazines being passed around at school.

Television introduced the boys to more than cowboys and the mysteries of girls. Along with the rest of the nation, Billy Ray and Bobby watched the increasing nightly news coverage of what would become the Vietnam War. Closer to home, Negroes were protesting. The boys saw the marchers, fires, riots, police dogs, and firehoses on TV, and wondered. These were the subjects of their riverside discussions now. For as long as Billy Ray and Bobby had been alive, "colored people" had had their own schools, their own water fountains, reserved seats on the bus—albeit in the back—private entrances and take-out windows at restaurants, and they got what Billy Ray and Bobby thought were the best seats at the show: the balcony. Colored folks were being *given* all those special privileges, so why were they marching and rioting? And what was going on in that far-away country they'd never heard of before? What was war really like? What had their fathers never told them? Was that why Bobby's father was sometimes angry, sometimes sad, and drank too much? Did the war have anything to do with Billy Ray's dad becoming a preacher?

Billy Ray's father's favorite song was "Amazing Grace." Every service would close with the congregation singing that song. Billy Ray also thought it was the most beautiful of all hymns, but he hated hearing it because, for reasons he didn't understand, it always made him want to cry. He had once told Bobby that he never wanted to hear the song again but would like it played at his funeral. It had been his father's favorite song because his father believed that by God's grace all souls would one day cross the river, metaphorically, to heaven. Billy Ray had believed that too, until Vietnam.

Tested

When they graduated from high school, Billy Ray and Bobby joined the Air Force Security Police. For one thing, they had always wanted to be cops. For another, it seemed a better option than being drafted by the Army or, God forbid, the Marines, and trudging through jungles and rice paddies on foot. They were right. Their entire year in Nam was at Tan San Nhut Air Base in Saigon. Neither ever fired his weapon at the enemy nor suffered any wound, except for Billy Ray's nightmare. Both of them returned to Georgia and joined their hometown police department. Because of their military police training and experience, they both had done well in the police academy.

Upon completion of the academy, rookie officers were assigned to a squad and rotated among veteran officers who served as informal field training officers and who saw their primary duty as teaching the rookies to forget everything the "dumb-asses" at the police academy had taught them and to retrain the rookies in the "right" way to "po-lice the streets."

Billy Ray's virgin ride as a cop was with Jarhead, rumored to be insane. The Sunday morning watch was quiet, and after about 2:00 a.m. the radio went silent. The city was asleep. Jarhead drove out a desolate county road and stopped at a sign that read "Warning: Entering Fort Benning, Property of the U.S. Government." Jarhead said nothing but got out and walked toward the rear of the blue-and-white patrol car. Billy Ray startled when Jarhead rapped on the window next to his head, motioning for him to get out. "You drive," Jarhead said. He had that deep, gravelly voice unique to Marine Corps drill instructors. Billy Ray got behind the wheel as Jarhead seated himself in the passenger seat. Billy Ray put the car in drive and began to make a U-turn when Jarhead barked, "Did I say turnaround?"

Billy Ray started, "No, but our jurisdiction ends here so I thought..."

"I don't give a dick about jurisdiction!" Jarhead nearly shouted. "Now drive, and fuck that sign, I hate signs!" A short time after entering the military reservation Jarhead said, "This is what you will do. You will increase our speed to sixty MPH and hold that speed. You will see a stop sign at a crossroad ahead, but you will *not* stop at the sign. You will go through the intersection at sixty. Are you clear?"

"Yes." Billy Ray tried to sound calm, thinking that maybe if there were no curves in either road he would be able to see any approaching cars. He increased speed to sixty. After a few minutes Jarhead said, "Turn off your headlights."

"What?" Billy Ray immediately regretted his instinctive question.

"Are you fucking deaf?" Jarhead yelled. Billy Ray turned off the lights. It took his eyes a moment to adjust, but he realized that there was sufficient moonlight for him to drive. He could now see the stop sign ahead. Jarhead asked, calmly,

"Are we at sixty?" Billy Ray confirmed this, and Jarhead rolled down his window as the stop sign seemed to grow. In quick, precise movements Jarhead reached for the Remington twelve gauge shotgun standing tall in the rack between the two officers, deftly unlocked it, grasped the wooden slide on the barrel with his left hand while guiding it out the window. His right hand moved to the trigger guard and he contorted his body so that his upper torso was leaning out the window. At maybe twenty yards from the sign Jarhead racked a round into the chamber and, nearly to the sign now, Billy Ray heard the shotgun's ominous blast as they flew through the intersection, Jarhead shouting, "Hot damn that was a rush!"

They went back to inspect the sign. Jarhead had obliterated the letter "P," but he was pissed, insisting he was aiming for the "O." Seeing Billy Ray's confused face, Jarhead said, "I told you, I fucking hate signs."

Jarhead got back behind the wheel, and they returned to their jurisdiction. At end-of-watch Jarhead said to him, "You passed the test." Billy Ray said nothing.

⌒

Bobby's introduction to Jarhead was quite different, but still a test of trust. Jarhead, who had said very little to Bobby as they prowled the streets, parked the car at Steffi's, a dingy bar in Benning Hills just outside the fort's main gate.

"Back me up," Jarhead said as they entered the bar. The patrons were a mix of veterans or retired soldiers embellishing stories of past glories and young, buzzed-head soldiers at Benning for boot camp or jump school. The young ones were full of piss and vinegar, suffering from a military-induced overdose of testosterone.

Being a cop, Jarhead didn't like anybody but cops, and being a Marine, he didn't like soldiers. They walked among the tables, Jarhead making eye contact with the drinkers, responding with only a slight nod to anyone acknowledging his presence. Bobby walked about six feet behind Jarhead. At a table of several shaved-heads Jarhead stopped abruptly, leaning forward until his face was only inches from one of the soldiers.

"What did you say?" Jarhead demanded.

"I didn't say anything to you!" the soldier replied, defiantly.

Jarhead exploded. "I heard you call me a son-of-a-bitch! Get up!" Jarhead shouted over the jukebox and the conversation. When the soldier hesitated, Jarhead grabbed the collar of his jacket, pulled him to his feet, and expertly pushed him out the door and to the side of the patrol car.

"Put your hands on the car and back up your feet!" Unhappy with the speed at which the soldier complied, Jarhead kicked the instep of his own foot against the soldier's, pushing the soldier's feet further back and putting him off balance, in position for a take-down if necessary.

"Search him," Jarhead said to Bobby, who had been standing back in a cover position. Bobby conducted a by-the-book search, as he had been taught in the academy, and finding no contraband, said "He's clean."

"Turn around," Jarhead said to the soldier. "Don't you ever…"

"I didn't…" the soldier tried to interrupt but was cut off.

"Shut the fuck up! Did I ask you anything, scumbag?" The soldier, clearly shaken now, snapped to attention and said, "Yes sir!" his rattled nerves confusing the police officer with his drill instructor.

"You are a guest in this city; and you will show respect to its police officers, do you understand?"

"Yes sir," replied the soldier, who was then "dismissed" by Jarhead and returned to his buddies with a tale to tell.

After the soldier walked away, Bobby said to Jarhead, "I didn't hear him say anything." Jarhead grinned like a psychopath. "That's because he didn't say shit. I was just fucking with him. But him and his buddies—who are listening to his tale as we speak—got the message: Don't fuck with the po-lice."

Jarhead looked at Bobby. "And you backed me up." Bobby had passed the test.

⁓

Billy Ray's training ride with Officer Johnson didn't begin well. The black man approached him, hand outstretched, and introduced himself, saying, "I be Johnson." Billy Ray, wanting to join in the humor, shook hands and replied, "I be Billy Ray." Johnson recoiled slightly and replied testily, "Fuck you, that's all worn out man," as Jarhead and the other veteran cops laughed uproariously. Officer Johnson's name was Isaiah Benjamin, and he went by his initials, I. B.

I. B. was handsome, fit, and "dapper" as Jarhead would say. He was well-liked and a competent police officer. The zone Billy Ray's squad covered was mostly poor and included several majority-black housing projects. The area was not completely segregated, though, largely because it bordered Fort Benning, and the Army had a better record of integration than the South. Still, there were large areas where the residents were nearly all black. I. B.'s beat was one such area, and it bordered what would become Billy Ray's beat.

It was the morning watch, and city ordinance required bars to close at 2:00 a.m. Just before that time, I. B. pulled the patrol car into the dark, crowded parking lot of a bar on a remote road. "You got my back," I. B. said, walking toward the building. Billy Ray had been in other bars and had seen the great dislike for cops in the eyes of the drinkers, but in this bar, on these black faces, he saw pure hate. It was no secret that many blacks hated cops. What had surprised Billy Ray was that they hated black cops more than white ones. Black cops were traitors. Billy Ray also knew by now that black cops tended to treat black suspects more harshly than did white cops. Another surprise.

Billy Ray trailed about six feet behind I. B., constantly swiveling his head to scan the area behind them. I. B. stopped to talk with a pretty young woman; they smiled and laughed. A few minutes later, I. B. left the bar, Billy Ray still following. "You drive," I. B. said. Two hours later, after the bars had closed and the streets had been swept of drunk drivers, I. B. directed him to a quiet, residential street, where they stopped in front of a small house.

"You go park the car somewhere nearby, in the dark. We get a call, you answer it, then come back and get me, I'll have my walkie. If there's no call, come back and get me in an hour."

Billy Ray pulled in front of the house an hour later. I. B. opened the front door, and Billy Ray could see the pretty woman from the bar inside the house. I. B. got into the patrol car. "Damn, that some good pussy!" he said. "Now let's go catch a burglar."

Billy Ray could only guess that the "test" was whether he would keep his mouth shut, and he did. I. B. was a smart man and a good cop, but he was married. Billy Ray concluded, that I. B., like too many men, was cursed with an inability to keep it in his pants. Billy Ray's father often said that "Idle hands are the Devil's workshop." Billy Ray decided that clearly applied to cops on the morning watch.

⌒

Niner's test for Billy Ray didn't come until he had completed field training and had his own beat and patrol car. The morning watch, again. The bars had closed, the streets cleared of drunks, and businesses checked for burglaries. It was time to play. Niner radioed him to meet at "Alpha," but that was a code known only to the two of them and intended to mislead supervisors as to their exact location. "Alpha" meant a place known as "Charlie." Niner and Billy Ray met at "Charlie" but left immediately, driving onto the Fort Benning reservation just off Victory Drive. Niner told him they were going to play "follow-the-leader." Billy Ray was told to turn off his headlights, stay two car lengths behind, and follow Niner no matter what.

They drove a short distance before turning into the parking lot of an elementary school, where they did several figure eights. Niner then drove onto the dimly lit walkway in front of the school, the cars barely squeezing between the school wall and the posts supporting the walkway's roof.

20 Allen Woods

Suddenly, Billy Ray saw the front of Niner's car drop as if off a cliff and the taillights jump so high that Billy Ray could see the undercarriage. In a split second, Niner's car was gone. Billy Ray thought about braking, but he had been told not to, so he braced himself for what might be at the bottom of the drop-off. His car pitched forward, almost slamming him against the steering wheel, and what he saw was Niner's car at the bottom of the drop-off, with the brake lights on! He raised his foot to brake but Niner's brake lights went dark as Niner gunned his engine and peeled to the right, avoiding a rear end collision by a second. When Billy Ray's car came to a stop, he sat a minute to compose himself. Niner walked up wearing a big, shit-eating grin. "Timed it just right, didn't I?"

Billy Ray had passed Niner's driving test.

Only one test remained for Billy Ray: his first solo arrest. He was dispatched to the Krystal burger joint on Victory Drive regarding a disorderly person. Billy Ray tried to talk to the drunken soldier, but the guy was a mean drunk and took a swing at him. Billy Ray dodged the swing and stepped forward, placing his right foot behind the drunk's and simultaneously striking him in the left side of the chest. The soldier tumbled to the ground, and Billy Ray pounced, rolling him onto his stomach and pulling one arm back. When the soldier resisted Billy Ray shoved his head into the pavement, warning him to cooperate. He got the soldier handcuffed, walked him to the patrol car, and put him in the back seat, behind the steel screen—"cuffed and stuffed." Billy Ray was surprised that none of his squad had come to back him up on his first arrest. Then, as he was about to get into his patrol car, he saw his sergeant's car pull slowly out from the shadows behind the Krystal. The sergeant, who had watched the entire arrest, pulled up beside him and said, simply, "You'll be OK."

"Well," Billy Ray replied, "the soldier was drunk."

"You'll do fine," the sergeant said, and drove away. Billy Ray was a cop.

Family

The Air Force had prepared Billy Ray and Bobby well for the structure of a police organization. What they hadn't expected was that the squad would become their family. Having been tested, found trustworthy, and accepted into their new family, it was not long before the veteran cops christened Billy Ray and Bobby with nicknames. The South, especially, has a tradition of nicknames, not always flattering. The region abounds with Bubbas, Skeeters, Docs, Cooters, and many others. The squad was no different.

Jarhead was Jarhead because he had been a Marine. Marines may call each other "Jarhead," but if the word comes out of the mouth of anyone other than a fellow Marine, the speaker best be prepared for a violent response. But Jarhead accepted the use of the nickname by his fellow cops because he considered them "brothers in blue." Jarhead was the real deal, a decorated Vietnam veteran awarded two bronze stars and two purple hearts. He was also, his brothers in blue had concluded, completely insane.

"Niner" arose, so-to-speak, from a peculiar daily physiological event experienced by that officer. Whenever an arrest was made on the morning watch, the arresting officer was required to appear in Recorder's Court that same morning to show probable cause for the arrest. Recorders Court was replete with characters who were nearly caricatures of themselves. It began at 8:00 a.m., often presided over by a grumpy old judge and a stone-faced police captain who acted as clerk-of-the-court, calling forward the accused, reciting the charges against the defendant, and administering an oath requiring all who would testify to tell the truth. All took the oath, many did not tell the truth.

Recorders Court could sometimes last for hours, depending on how many "scumbags" were arrested the night before. Therein lay the problem for Niner. All men on occasion experience a morning hard-on. Niner, however, had a *daily* morning erection. And it was not just daily but always at 9:00 a.m., regular as clockwork.

The first three rows of seats in Recorders Court were reserved for police officers, who were usually tired and irritable after being on duty all night. They all came awake, however, whenever Niner was called to testify just before nine o'clock. The cops would all watch the clock on the wall behind the judge; and at exactly nine, even if he were standing before the judge testifying, Niner would aim a sly grin toward the gallery of admiring officers, his boner bulging against his tight uniform trousers. The scene looked practically choreographed: three rows of cops would see Niner's expression, look up at the clock and then back to Niner's boner. At least for a moment, it felt that all was right with the otherwise fucked-up world.

The nickname, at first, had been Nine O'clock, but nine had been combined with boner to arrive at Niner. Other than Bobby, Niner would become Billy Ray's closest cop friend. He was, simply put, one of the smartest people Billy Ray had ever known, had a strange sense of humor, and was, quite possibly, insane—but weren't they all? They are, after all, the ones who rush *toward* gunfire.

The squad's sergeant didn't really have a nickname; he was simply Sarge. He had been a cop since he was twenty-one. In his late thirties, he had served as a patrol officer and undercover narcotics officer before being promoted to sergeant and returned to the patrol division. He was level-headed, knowledgeable, protected his officers as best he could from the sometimes unfair police bureaucracy, and was always there for them when they had personal problems. He was not just a manager, he was a leader. Even Jarhead admitted that Sarge was as good as any Marine sergeant he had known. Love is a word the tough cops would never have used in describing their sergeant, but it was accurate all the same.

Bobby was tall, slim, and movie-star handsome; girls swooned over him. Billy Ray attested that this had been true since middle school and that Bobby had always dated the most beautiful girls, rarely more than once or twice, so as "not to disappoint those he had not yet met," as Bobby would often quip. He would frequently drive the forty-five miles to Auburn University where the girls, according to Bobby, thought it was chic to date an "older" man, and a cop at that. Everyone was jealous of Bobby's beautiful girls. Jarhead once remarked to Billy Ray that Bobby "got more pussy than the Pope." It was Jarhead who, ultimately, had given Bobby his nickname. I. B. had once called Bobby "Pretty Boy Floyd." Jarhead shortened it, and Bobby became "Floyd" to everyone but Billy Ray.

As for Billy Ray, Jarhead tagged him "Preacher," and it had stuck. Billy Ray would not have chosen this, but nicknames are not usually chosen. The nickname was not because Billy Ray was religious, although he was. Rather, Jarhead called him Preacher because Billy Ray was a *believer.* He still believed in "right and wrong" and "good and evil." He still believed in the basic goodness of mankind. He believed in the law and in doing what was right. But Billy Ray hated his nickname. He knew he didn't deserve it, not after Vietnam.

Preacher

His father had preached about the clear line between right and wrong, but after becoming a cop, Billy Ray learned that the line was often quite thin. The law allowed the police to use only the "minimum force necessary" to make an arrest; and any force beyond that was "excessive force." But cops distinguished between *excessive* force and what they might call *unnecessary* force. Unnecessary force was, indeed, beyond the minimum force allowed by law but did not cross the line to brutality, or what the cops thought of as excessive force. Unnecessary force was wrong, illegal, and Bobby Ray resisted it, aware that society needed the doctrine of minimum force. But he would learn that, while necessary, it was a doctrine preached by fools and hypocrites.

His own resolve to honor the doctrine first failed him on a busy evening watch. He had arrested a drunk driver and wife-beater who earlier the same night had sent his wife to the hospital and fled the scene. The drunk was handcuffed behind his back and in the back seat, separated by the heavy-duty steel mesh screen that protected officers from scumbags. This particular scumbag puked in the patrol car, then started hollering, threatening to sue him and swearing at him with every curse he could remember. Then he cursed Preacher's mother, made a guttural sound, and spat a huge ball of phlegm onto the back of Preacher's head.

"Dog!" Preacher shouted and slammed hard on the breaks, throwing the drunk, hands cuffed behind him and not belted in, forward and slamming his face into the wire mesh. There was no dog, of course. Preacher had just conducted a "screen test," clearly an act of unnecessary force, though not, by cop definition, an act of excessive force. The screen had passed the test, having protected him from the projectile drunk. At the booking desk at the jail the grizzled old sergeant looked over his glasses at the diamond-shaped pattern of red marks on one side of the suspect's face but said nothing; neither did the drunk. Preacher would learn that many suspects, especially drunks who committed acts they would never commit sober, believed they deserved what they got and would not file a complaint.

Privately, Preacher realized that unnecessary force was often the result of frustration, fatigue, or anger, and sometimes the motive was simple revenge: "You hit us, and we'll hit you harder." He thought about sports and sportsmanship, or the lack of it—a major league pitcher hits a batter in one inning, and in the next the other team's pitcher hits another batter, or the round-baller who delivers an elbow to the face of an opponent who had aggressively fouled a teammate, and who would even watch hockey if not for the fouls and retaliatory fights? Sure, police represented the government and should be held to a higher standard, but a zero-tolerance policy on unnecessary force denied the humanity of cops. This is what Billy Ray thought, but he talked about abiding by the law and made an effort to restrain his own instinct to hit back as best he could and even tactfully intervened to prevent unnecessary force by others. He was Preacher.

The Good, the Bad, and the Bullshit

Preacher and Floyd settled into the life of cops. After six months they became regulars at "choir practice." Cops always gathered at end-of-watch to ruminate over and tell stories about that day's calls, relaxing with the aid of beer or something stronger. Preacher caught the irony of the phrase, but he didn't know its origin until someone finally told him to read *The Choir Boys*, a novel by a former cop. Choir practice was a time to unload the stress of the job with others who knew first-hand the dark underbelly of humanity. It was a kind of therapy, with self-medication. It was also the forge that formed the strong bonds between them. The officers loved their families and believed they had to protect them from the scumbags, but they talked more to each other than they did to their spouses, which was reflected in the high divorce rate in Preacher's squad and every other. At choir practice the cops told stories about the boredom, the bullshit, and, sometimes, the horror. These were stories that stayed with Preacher; he thought about them often, sometimes driving his patrol car down near the old Chattahoochee boat ramp where he and Bobby used to fish and think. He was sure these stories would haunt him until the end of his life.

There was the fool who, desperate to lose weight so a woman he fancied would date him, chained himself to a tree, locked the chain with a padlock, and threw the key into the bushes. He attracted attention after dark, yelling "Help me, I'm starving to death!" The chain was cut and the man rescued. Jarhead, having recently attended crisis counseling training, made an effort to comply with the chief's directive for officers to be more sensitive. "Sir, you have my sympathy," he said to the hopeless, weeping man, "but if you want the bitch to fuck you, you gotta stop eating like a pig!"

One night he and Niner entered an apartment to serve an arrest warrant. Upon opening the door and seeing cops, the suspect turned and ran, but Niner tackled him and the struggle was on. Preacher and Niner and the suspect were all entangled on the floor, the two cops trying in only the dim light of an aquarium to get the man's hands behind his back to cuff him. "Twist his foot," Niner shouted to Preacher. Preacher grabbed a foot in the darkness and twisted as hard as he could. "Ow, that's *my* foot!" Niner hollered. Preacher laughed; he couldn't help it. Then Niner started laughing, and even the suspect laughed so hard he could no longer resist.

Staying awake all night and sleeping during the day is not natural, but is part of the job for many cops. Falling asleep on the morning watch was not uncommon and was another source of funny stories. There was the time Niner failed to answer dispatch. Preacher had talked to Niner a short time before and knew he had planned to check for burglaries behind a strip mall on Victory Drive. Preacher drove behind the mall and saw Niner's car, headlights out, spotlight shining on the building. Niner had been driving slowly and simply fallen asleep at the wheel. The car had stopped upon hitting a bump in the road.

Preacher had himself once fallen asleep while stopped at a red light. Niner had pulled up behind him, sitting through three cycles of the light before blasting Preacher awake with his siren.

Then there was the unfortunate officer who fell asleep while driving and crashed into a parked train. He was moving so slowly the only injury was to his pride, and that would only get worse. Ever after the officer's nickname was Choo-Choo, and whenever he was on the morning watch after that someone would key a mic during the early morning hours and everyone on the radio would hear, "Choo...Choo, Choo...Choo."

Of course, people do more than sleep at night. As Preacher

was patrolling one night, Jarhead radioed him to "switch to four," which was code to switch to channel *three*, which might grant a second without supervisors hearing. Jarhead then said, "Meet me at that other place," another code. Preacher arrived at "that other place," a remote wooded area, to see a civilian car and Jarhead's patrol car, engine running, windows fogged so that Preacher couldn't see inside. Both of the back doors of Jarhead's car were closed. Preacher immediately knew what had happened. As he approached the patrol car, a hand wiped away condensation from the rear window, and he could see Jarhead's face and naked chest at the window; behind Jarhead he could see a nude stripper he recognized from a bar on Jarhead's beat. Preacher couldn't help but laugh at Jarhead's pissed-off face.

"This ain't funny, asshole!" Jarhead shouted. Preacher mustered his most hurt and indignant expression. "Asshole? Fuck you, Jarhead," Preacher said, then turned and walked away, Jarhead's curses growing fainter with each step. He got into his patrol car and drove off, grinning to himself. Jarhead would have left a back door open, but it was cold. The woman must have closed it. Of course, there are no inside handles on the back doors of police cars, and they couldn't get into the front seat—where they had left their clothes—because of the security screen. Fortunately for Jarhead, he had taken his walkie into the back seat. Five minutes later Jarhead called Preacher again and advised him to switch channels, again by code, then asked, very politely, "One-oh-three, could you handle that detail for me now?" He did.

⌒

Inevitably, for Preacher, remembering the good stories led to remembering the bad, and there were far too many of those.

One hot, humid night Preacher had gotten a call about a five-year-old girl who hadn't come home for dinner. He cruised the poor neighborhood where the girl lived; it was not uncommon for young kids to be seen walking alone. He talked mostly to kids, while the missing girl's mother and siblings waited in the house, in the air conditioning. No one had seen the girl, and the sun was slowly lowering in the western sky, across the river, over Alabama. He returned to the house, called for assistance from the Juvenile Detective Office, and began interviewing the mother and brothers for a first responder report. He knew the older brother, eighteen, because he had once arrested the kid for marijuana possession. None of the family was able to provide any information about the little girl beyond her basic description. Her mother couldn't remember what clothes she was wearing; she hadn't seen the little girl much that day. When he interviewed the other brother, half-brother actually, the fifteen-year-old watched cartoons throughout the interview and seemed to Preacher to be…what? Indifferent? Detached? He passed his impression along to the detective; later he would realize that that was the first time he felt he had a good instinct as a cop.

The search ended that night but continued the next day. The girl's minister was the one who found her. The house backed up to a wooded area in the flood plain of the Chattahoochee that had once been an area dredged for sand to use elsewhere. Digging out the sand had left "borrow pits" that filled with water, creating numerous small ponds throughout the woods. The girl was floating face down in the middle of one of the ponds. When the other searchers responded to the minister's alert they found the minister sitting on the edge of the pond, sobbing uncontrollably.

It was not an accidental drowning. The girl's fifteen

year old half-brother had raped her, sodomized her both orally and anally, tied her hands behind her back, and thrown her into the pond to drown. Preacher imagined the last thoughts of her short life, a mix of betrayal, confusion, pain, and that desperate fear that accompanies the inability to breathe. He wondered how the minister would explain God's will to his flock.

That call had been a bad one, but hardly his first tragedy. Riding with Niner as his training officer, they had been dispatched to the shooting of a two-year-old. Niner was the best driver Preacher had ever seen, but that didn't keep Billy Ray's knuckles from turning white in their grip on the armrest or his knees from aching as his feet pressed hard against the fire wall while, siren blasting and blue lights flashing, Niner passed cars on the right, in the emergency lane, at *one hundred* miles an hour, intermittently weaving between startled drivers who never knew whether to move right, left, or slam on their brakes. Anticipating what drivers would do was the skill that divided cops, like Niner, who would arrive safely at their destination from those who would die or, perhaps worse, kill innocent citizens. Preacher and Niner arrived safely.

But the baby was dead, shot by her father with an "empty" handgun he was cleaning. One life lost, another cursed with unfathomable grief and guilt. And for Niner and Preacher, another unwanted memory, this one of blood and brains and a lifeless little body.

It was Bobby who caught "the Devil call." Preacher was back-up. The dispatcher gave the code for unknown problem and advised Bobby to switch to the secure channel four; then she advised that the caller was a hysterical female babbling something about the Devil and her daughter, a "possible ten-seventy-four." Bobby arrived first and entered the living room, where he saw a young black woman, maybe twenty-five, sitting on a sofa, rocking back and forth, crying, repeating, "The Devil did it, the Devil did it." Bobby asked, "The Devil did what?" She continued to rock, cry, and repeat the same refrain, but she pointed to a bedroom door. Bobby entered the room, clearly a child's room. In a corner, sitting, no, slumping in a chair was a girl, maybe twelve, head back, eyes open and staring as if she really had seen the Devil. The girl was naked from the waist down, her legs were spread wide, and a bloody broom handle protruded from her vagina, the straw end resting on the floor in a large pool of blood.

Preacher arrived as Bobby's back-up. Bobby had also called for a homicide detective. When the detective arrived, Bobby volunteered to stay with the suspect, so Preacher and the detective entered the crime scene room. They both stopped dead. The detective said he needed something from his car and excused himself. Preacher stood there a moment, alone in the room, staring at the girl, feeling bile rise from his stomach into his throat. He strode quickly through the living room, outside and around to the side of the house where he immediately joined the veteran detective in puking up his lunch. Ordinarily, a cop puking at a crime scene was certain to warrant a great amount of ribbing. Not this time. Neither the detective, nor Bobby—who had quickly puked in the toilet and flushed it before anybody else arrived—nor Preacher would ever speak of their sickness.

The investigation revealed that the drug-addicted mother had accused her twelve-year-old daughter of dressing like a "ho" and "tempting mens." In a drug-induced psychosis, the mother had become convinced that the Devil was in her daughter and making her "act a ho." The mother had repeatedly and forcefully thrust the broom handle into her daughter's vagina in an effort to drive out the Devil and "save" the girl. Further investigation revealed that the mother's drug-addicted, live-in, thirty-year-old boyfriend had been raping the girl for six months. Indeed, the Devil had been in her daughter.

I. B.

It was a quiet Monday morning watch. The squad was gathered in a clearing in Benning Hills, surrounded by thick woods and accessible by a single dirt road, for an on-duty "choir practice" that included no alcohol and was attended by supervisors, including the watch captain. It was a pizza party; the pizzas, being those cooked but not sold by the time Victory Pizza Place closed, were provided gratis. The patrol cars were backed into a circle like the wagon trains of old. Cops sat on the trunks of their patrol cars, sharing pizza and conversation. Jarhead had turned on a portable radio, playing country music from station WDAQ, which they all listened to primarily because of the late night disc jockey, "Suzy-Q." Her sweet, soothing voice was comforting, and they all loved her. Some had actually dated her, but they all considered her their friend, an honor not bestowed on many not wearing blue.

A song ended, and as Suzy-Q began to talk, Jarhead hushed the group. "Listen up!" Suzy-Q continued, "This next song was requested by one of our boys-in-blue out there keeping us all safe tonight," at which Jarhead pounded his chest with both fists, grunting, "Ooh-rah!"

"Here's George Strait," said Suzy, spinning the country crooner's hit song, "All My Exes Live in Texas." They all listened in silence until Jarhead sang along loudly with the final chorus, "All my exes live in Texas, and Texas is the place I'd truly love to be, but all my exes live in Texas, that's why I reside in Tennessee."

"Fuck Texas!" Jarhead declared.

"Ain't you from Texas, Jarhead?" Niner asked.

"Damn right I'm from Texas, where everything is bigger, and I'll show you my dick if you don't believe that!" His offer was met with a loud chorus of decline. Jarhead added, "Texas is big, but it ain't big enough for both me and my third ex."

They all laughed, but their laughter was interrupted by the radio, "One-oh-three and one-oh-one."

"One-oh-three go ahead," Preacher responded. The dispatcher gave an address and the code, "Seventy-four-ten"—a shooting. His heart pounded.

"One-oh-three clear." Sarge saw the look in Preacher's eyes.

"What is it, Preacher?"

"That's I. B.'s address." I. B. was off that night. There was a mad scramble as the squad scattered into six patrol cars and raced down the dirt road, becoming a flashing blue dragon howling through the city's streets.

The front door was open; they entered with guns drawn. Preacher was the first in because it was his call. Nothing in the living room. Clear. He heard loud crying from a bedroom. He braced against the wall, the others lined up behind him, then, with gun and eyes, he took a quick peek into the room. He saw I. B. lying on the floor, eyes open and staring in shock, blood puddling from his neck. I. B.'s wife, Mavis, was sitting on the bed, his police gun in her hand. She had known that I. B. cheated on her, but this was different; he had taken another woman into *her* bed. Preacher pointed his gun directly at her, praying she wouldn't make him shoot her.

"Mavis, put the gun down on the floor." She looked up at him, frightening Preacher with her hesitation. But then she leaned forward, placed the gun on the floor, and sat up straight. The situation was stabilized, Mavis was cuffed, and the paramedics were working on I. B.

As always when a cop is shot, a vigil of cops gathered outside the emergency room, waiting for word. Word soon came that I. B. would live. The hammer dropped the next day, when word spread that I. B. was "a cabbage," paralyzed from the neck down, with no hope of recovery. As soon as possible, they all visited I. B. in the hospital and assured him they would see him when he returned home. I. B. did return home, because he refused to press charges against Mavis, and some cops did visit. I. B.'s house was on Preacher's beat, and he had stopped by once. He meant to do so again, he really did, but he didn't.

Preacher did see I. B. again, though. Less than a year later he was dispatched to the house on an eighty-two-hundred call, a domestic disturbance. Sarge had recognized the address and advised dispatch that he would back up one-oh-three. I. B.'s six-year-old son opened the door; Preacher would learn later from the dispatcher that it was the boy who had called 911, saying, "My mommy's hurting my daddy."

Mavis was shouting, "I can't stay here all the time. I'm going crazy! I'm a young woman. I need a man to fuck me, and you ain't no man." Preacher told the boy to go to his room and close the door. He entered I. B.'s bedroom, which was now I. B.'s entire world, and saw him lying in his hospital bed, tears streaming down his cheeks. The stench of stale urine overwhelmed the room; the urine bag hanging from the bed was overflowing into a large puddle on the floor.

Mavis turned her attention to Preacher. "Get out," she snarled. "I didn't call you!"

Preacher pointed at the urine bag. "Fix it!" he ordered through clenched teeth. Mavis started to say something but he took a step toward her, stuck his finger in her face, and commanded, "Shut the fuck up, Mavis, and fix this!"

While Mavis was changing the bag and mopping up the urine from the floor, he reached out and took I. B.'s hand into his, a gesture he immediately realized as foolish, because I.

B. could not feel it. Sarge had arrived and was standing in the doorway. *Cops were supposed to fix things*, Preacher thought. People call, we come, and we fix the problem. Preacher couldn't fix this. He felt helpless and angry.

When Mavis finished cleaning up, Preacher told her to go into the living room and wait for him there. He said to I. B., "OK, buddy, we got this fixed. I'm going to talk to Mavis and see that it doesn't happen again." More tears from I. B. Preacher wondered if they ever stopped. He and Sarge each made eye contact with I. B., nodded, and left the room.

In the living room, Mavis backed away from the rage in Preacher's eyes until her back was against the wall. Defiance welled up in her. "What the fuck do you expect?" she demanded. "All the motherfucker does is lay there and shit and piss!"

Preacher filled his lungs and took a step forward. His nose was one inch from hers, their eyes locked in hatred, when he felt Sarge's hand on his shoulder, a gentle human touch, a reminder to remain human, not to slip across that very fine line into insanity. He raised his right hand.

"Go ahead, beat me," Mavis said. "I know you want to."

He did want to, but he had never hit a woman in anger. Instead, his voice lowered to a threatening murmur, "If we *ever* come here again and find him like that, you will lose your children and go to jail for a very long time. Do you understand me?" She nodded. He stepped away then and radioed, "Ten-eight," back in service.

No one in the squad would see I. B. alive again; he died of an infection a few months after the domestic disturbance call. The medical examiner ruled that I. B. had died of natural causes, but Preacher wondered if Mavis had found a way to kill I. B. by infection. Was it murder? Or homicide? And if Mavis had killed I. B., was it a mercy killing? I. B., a good friend, a good cop, a horrible trauma, a too-early death… Preacher would file it away, no time to grieve now.

There was a choir practice to honor I. B., with shared stories, shared silence, and too many shared spirits. When it seemed all the stories had been told and quiet engulfed the officers, Jarhead said, "I'd like to propose a toast to I. B." They were all surprised, because Jarhead never said anything positive about anybody; still, they answered with several hearty calls of "hear, hear." Raising his beer can, Jarhead said,

"To I. B., a good man, a good cop, our brother-in-blue"…here and there someone responded with a *yes* or an *amen*…before Jarhead continued, "and a damn good jigaboo." Jarhead was met with a ragged chorus of *Fuck you, Jarhead!* and several flying beer cans.

"What?" asked Jarhead, genuinely confused.

"9000"

Life moved on, six months of relative calm. It was shift-change. The patrol cars ran twenty-four hours a day, passed on from one watch to the next. Three-oh-three, the evening watch, which ended at midnight, had had a late call, so Preacher was late getting his car. He was just about to leave headquarters when he got the call, "One-oh-three," and responded, "One-oh-three, go ahead." The dispatcher gave him the name and address of a convenience store on his beat and the code, "Seventy-three-hundred," an armed robbery alarm call. It was an "alarm" call because the cash register had one rigged drawer that would activate an alarm in police dispatch whenever the twenty dollar bill in that drawer was removed. The police would be alerted early in the robbery without the robber knowing. The only problem was that the often young, unskilled, and poorly trained clerks would forget and pull the alarm bill from the register, resulting in many false alarms, and, supervisors feared, officer complacency. Preacher responded, "One-oh-three clear, leaving headquarters," letting the dispatcher and any other officers who might be closer to the store know that he was a long way off.

Sarge, who had left headquarters quickly and was closer to the call than Preacher, radioed in, "Eighty-one will take that seventy-three-hundred."

"Ten-four, sergeant, thank you," the dispatcher replied. Supervisors were not routinely dispatched to calls, and dispatchers sincerely appreciated it when they volunteered. Preacher knew from talking with dispatchers over the years that they also are dedicated officers and often feel the burden of responsibility when they can't get help to someone quickly, even though they don't control the number of officers on the street.

Preacher was en route when he heard Sarge report "Ten-ninety-seven," arrived on the scene. The dispatcher hit an emergency buzzer that blared into all patrol cars and said,

"All units standby," an instruction to keep that channel clear until the unit responding to the high-risk situation radioed in an "all clear." It had been too long since Sarge's arrival, and suddenly, just as Preacher approached the store, the radio erupted with a loud, frantic voice, "One-oh-five to headquarters, nine-thousand, nine-thousand!" Officer down.

Preacher entered the store with gun drawn. The one-oh-five officer was standing over Sarge, who was lying on his back on the floor, his gun still in its holster, with blood pooled around his head. There was no one else in the store. He radioed headquarters, "One-oh-three to headquarters make that 10-43 (ambulance) 10-18 (quickly), this is a headshot." He said to the other officer, "Check in the back for some towels," but the officer replied that she had a first aid kit in her car and went for it. Preacher kneeled beside Sarge, who was breathing raspy, irregular breaths. There was bloody foam around his mouth, and Preacher could see bits of brain matter in the blood pool. He pushed Sarge's hair back from his forehead and could clearly see the hole where the bullet entered the left side of the forehead. He raised Sarge's head slightly so he could slide his hand underneath and feel for the exit hole. It wasn't difficult to find; it was not the neat, small, round hole like on the forehead. He covered both holes with his hands until the other officer returned with the medical kit. Preacher applied several gauze pads to both wounds and the other officer wrapped gauze around Sarge's head to hold the pads in place. He continued to apply pressure to both wounds until paramedics arrived. Sarge was alive when they took him away, but not for long.

Preacher sat on the curb in the parking lot as crime scene technicians did their jobs and detectives pieced together what happened. Sarge was not one to be complacent, and he had not been, not really. Before Sarge arrived, the robber had locked several customers and the store clerk in the cooler in the rear of the store. The robber had also taken the clerk's smock and put it on. When Sarge arrived, he undoubtedly approached the store cautiously from the side, so he could peer into the store without exposing himself to the front glass wall. He may even have drawn his gun while doing that, but looking inside, what he saw was a young, black male wearing the store smock and standing behind the counter. That scene would lead one to believe the call was a false alarm. He entered the store, walked to the counter, and the robber raised a gun from behind the counter, firing one round that struck Sarge in the head as he attempted to duck.

The lieutenant, seeing Preacher sitting on the curb, hands bloodied, asked him if he wanted to go home for the remainder of the watch.

"No, can I go inside and wash the blood off now?"

"Yeah, it's cleared inside; and if you don't want to go home then let's get out there and find this son-of-a-bitch."

Preacher didn't just want to find the murderer, he wanted to kill him. For the first time in his life, Preacher *wanted* to kill a man. He wasn't alone: every cop on duty that night hoped for the opportunity to kill the scumbag cop-killer who had killed one of their family, one of their brothers. Preacher patrolled dark alleys, parked his car and walked down darkened streets, getting down on his hands and knees, gun in hand, to look under cars, and went to every abandoned building he could think of, searching with his flashlight. He had become a predator, searching for a kill. But it was not to be. The suspect was arrested by other officers just before end-of-watch. The suspect, like many cowards, would ambush a cop but not give the cops a reason to kill him legally when arrested. The suspect, the "man" who had murdered Sarge, was fifteen years old. His youth only made Preacher angrier that the arresting officers had not killed him, because society would not have the guts to execute him due to his "tender age."

This would be Preacher's fourth cop funeral. Two officers had been killed during robberies some years before, then there was I. B.'s funeral, and now Sarge. Cop funerals are pure hell for cops. They do put on good funerals though. Sarge, in his late thirties, had been a cop since he was twenty-one. He had friends in many departments and state and federal agencies. The procession of police cars, blue lights flashing, from the funeral at the church to the interment at the cemetery, was more than a mile long. Funerals were always sad, but it was the burials that Preacher found most difficult. In particular, the presentation of a tri-folded American flag to Sarge's grieving widow, surrounded by her confused children, nearly gutted him. Then there were the bagpipes. How can their awful, wailing sounds illicit such emotion? Preacher held it together until the final piping, "Amazing Grace." That melody, as it always did, brought tears that rolled down both cheeks as he said goodbye to a good man, a good cop, a good friend, and a brother-in-blue.

Preacher would file away much of his grief over Sarge in that cavern in his mind that held things to be dealt with later. The blood stains in the knees of his uniform trousers were not as easy to ignore. Despite numerous washings, the stains remained a constant reminder of kneeling in that puddle of Sarge's blood and brain matter. Finally Preacher scissored the trousers into dozens of pieces and discarded them. Then he had to reimburse the department for a replacement pair.

Preacher knew from Vietnam that trauma could result in recurring nightmares, and he was not immune. His periodic nightmare from the trauma of Sarge's death was not a replay of the images he had seen that night; it was not about Sarge's death—it was about his own. In the nightmare he would walk into a small convenience store that was on his beat, near the one in which Sarge was killed, and as he approached the counter the clerk would raise a double-barreled shotgun and blast a hole in his guts. The noise of the shotgun always woke him. Once, in waking life, he steeled himself and, hand on his gun, walked into the real store, thinking that doing so and not being shot might end the nightmares. It didn't work. He was fortunate, though, in that the nightmare recurred only periodically and ended a few months after Sarge's death. The Vietnam nightmare, however, stayed.

No Stress

Cops got an occasional respite from their routine when the department would send them to the Georgia Police Academy in Atlanta for in-service training. Following Sarge's death, somebody in headquarters thought it would be a good idea to send the squad to a new training course titled "Stress for Police." They were sent one or two at the time; Preacher was teamed to attend with Jarhead, who immediately deemed it a "stupid fucking class" because it was not named "Less Stress for Police."

The instructor was a psychologist. Preacher found her to be sincere, caring, and full of real compassion for police officers, and he thought she offered some helpful strategies for combating stress. Jarhead concluded that she was "a pointy-headed intellectual, liberal, idealist who thought a group hug would fix everything and who didn't know a goddamned thing about the real world." Jarhead made it clear to classmates that he would not be participating in any "fucking group hug" but added that he did think the psychologist had a nice ass and that he would be happy to fuck her if that would make everything better.

The courses at the academy were open to any law enforcement agency in the state, and therein lay the best reason for going there: meeting officers from police departments around the state. At the stress course Preacher and Jarhead befriended an Atlanta narcotics officer named Marco, who, almost inevitably, was nicknamed Marco-Narco by Jarhead. On the last night of class they all gathered for drinks, stories, lies, and goodbyes. Marco then took Preacher and Jarhead to several of Atlanta's finer strip joints, where they sat front-row, watching nearly nude women writhing to sexual music. Occasionally one of them would slide a dollar bill into a stripper's garter. The women weren't completely naked: breasts could be legally displayed but vaginas could not. *Who decides this shit?* Preacher wondered.

At the last club they visited, Marco, who, being a narcotics officer, knew many characters in Atlanta's underworld, invited a stripper he knew to "party" with them after the joint closed. They soon found themselves in Grant Park, home of the Atlanta Zoo, picnic areas, and the famous Cyclorama, a huge circular mural and diorama depicting the Civil War Battle of Atlanta. The park was in a high-crime area, and it was against the law to enter the park after closing, but they were the law. Preacher and Marco sat beneath an observation tower, drinking and conducting a mini-choir practice while Jarhead and the stripper were up in the observation deck doing…whatever they were doing.

When Jarhead and the stripper came down, they all left the park, took the stripper home, and headed back to the hotel, but, being drunk, they took a wrong turn. Marco stopped the unmarked car and slurred, "Oh shit, we're on Moreland Avenue." They were the only white dudes in the heart of Atlanta's murder capital. Somewhat sobered by their predicament, Marco pulled his gun from its holster and laid it on the seat for quick access. Following Marco's lead, Preacher did the same.

"Oh, shit!" Jarhead exclaimed from the back seat. He had reached for his gun and found it wasn't there. He had left his gun *and* his badge in the observation tower in Grant Park. They got off Moreland Avenue as quickly as possible, sped back to the park, hoping—Preacher wondered if Jarhead might even be praying—that the gun and badge would still be there. Losing a gun or badge induced a kind of shame that was difficult for an officer to overcome, regardless of the circumstances. Jarhead was lucky. The gun and badge were where he had left them.

"So much for coming to Atlanta to relieve our fucking stress!" said Jarhead. They had, however, formed a strong bond with their new brother, Marco-Narco.

A House of Cards

Their schedule was six-on-three-off, so they sometimes had a weekend off. With such a weekend coming up, Preacher called Bobby to make plans, but Bobby already had a date with another co-ed at Auburn and said he would be there the entire weekend. Tough life, Preacher thought. It had only been about four months since stress training; feeling the need to get out of town, Preacher called Marco-Narco, who said he had to work but also said he could get permission for a courtesy ride-a-long and that it might be fun. So, Atlanta it would be for Preacher.

He sat in on the planning briefing. The target for the night would be a queer club, The Pink Mushroom, in the Piedmont Park area. Atlanta had a large homosexual population that was generally ignored by the police unless there were complaints about drugs, and there had been complaints about the "Pink Shroom." The plan was simple. Marco explained to his squad that their guest, Preacher, would go in first, scope out the place, go into the bathroom and radio the intelligence back to Marco. Preacher would have an ear piece so he could hear the radio traffic between Marco and his team.

The front door team was in place in a van down the street from the bar. The back door team was in route but had been delayed. Marco sent Preacher in. The bar was dimly lit with a soft pink hue. The music was low and sensual as several couples, all men, slow-danced in a small open area. With the exception of one couple at the bar, who were engrossed in kissing, all eyes seemed to be on Preacher, fresh meat. As he passed the kissing couple, whose hands were on each other's crotch, they ended the kiss and one glanced at him.

Time seemed to freeze as Preacher and Bobby stared into each other's eyes.

Bobby, eyes wide and mouth agape, tried to speak first but managed only "I…" before losing his voice.

"What the fuck?" is what had come out of Preacher's mouth involuntarily. The man Bobby had been kissing, with an open hand on the side of his face and looking aghast that there might be a scene, said, in a very effeminate voice, "And who might you be?"

Preacher turned to the queer, looked him in the eyes and said in a voice full of threat, "Shut the fuck up, and take a walk, now!" The queer moved his hand from his cheek to his heart and said, "Sorry, he said he wasn't *with* anyone," and walked away, exiting the bar, thank God.

Preacher grabbed Bobby's arm without looking at him. "Come with me." He dragged Bobby from the stool and guided him out the back door of the bar. He had not heard the back door narcotics team announce their arrival on the radio and he prayed they would not be there yet. Outside, Bobby started to talk but Preacher cut him off.

"Where are you staying?" Bobby gave him a hotel name

and room number. Preacher told Bobby the bar was about to be raided and to get the hell out of the area as quickly as possible.

The raid was uneventful but not, for Preacher, inconsequential. His mind could not clear the unreal scene of Bobby kissing a queer, because it *was* real. He excused himself as soon as possible after the debriefing, telling Marco he wasn't feeling well, and headed for Bobby's hotel. When he arrived, Bobby was sitting on one of the two beds, leaning forward, head in hands. Billy Ray sat down on the other bed, across from Bobby, and said, "Talk to me, Bobby."

"There's nothing to talk about, really, I'm a queer," replied Bobby, now sobbing.

"That's crazy talk," Preacher said. "What about all the women you've fucked over the years, the girls at Auburn, hell, the girls in high school; queers don't fuck women!"

"You don't get it!" Bobby almost shouted. "There were no girls in high school, no co-eds at Auburn! The reason I never dated girls more than twice is because I was *not* fucking them. I've never been attracted to girls. I've known I was queer since I was ten years old. I've *never* fucked a woman."

Bobby's last comment took Preacher's mind back to Vietnam. "That's bullshit," he said. "You fucked that girl in Nam, we all did!" Bobby shook his head in frustration, replying, "No, no, no, I didn't fuck the girl in Nam, nobody fucked *that* girl but you!" Bobby immediately regretted his words.

Preacher sat very still, trying to square what Bobby had just said with his memory, reliving that night in Nam that so often came to him as a nightmare. His buddies, Bobby and two other airmen, had taken turns with the whore, and he was last, after Bobby. He didn't remember going into the room; the nightmare was what he remembered when he "woke up" in the whorehouse. The flashing red strobe light, the slower than normal movement of everything, and especially the young Vietnamese pimp, a boy of maybe sixteen screaming, "You kill sister, you kill sister!" Lying next to Billy Ray was a young girl, no older than the boy, and God forbid, probably younger, possibly three or four years younger, her eyes closed, motionless, legs spread, with blood stains on the sheet underneath her hips. It all seemed to him like some strange dream, the result of the hallucinogen his buddies had slipped into his drink earlier. Bobby and his other buddies had burst into the room, taking in the sight of the girl and the blood. Now the pimp was yelling, "I call MP, I call MP!" One of his buddies hit the hysterical pimp with a hard right cross, knocking him out. Bobby and the others pulled Preacher from the bed, helped him get his clothes on, and rushed him away. In the days that followed they heard no rumors of a dead whore, but the ruling American emperor in Vietnam, MAC-V (Military Assistance Command–Vietnam) censored the news and covered-up wrong-doing by Americans in order to maintain good relations with the people of South Vietnam in general, and Saigon in particular.

His buddies had admitted slipping the hallucinogenic mickey into his drink, but their story had always been that they had each fucked the girl, who was *not* dead because his two buddies had seen her move before they fled the scene of, what, the crime? Had there been a crime?

"You're not making sense," Preacher said, "I saw each of you going into the girl's room." Bobby covered his eyes with his hands, stood, and walked across the room. Still reeling from being so abruptly outed to the only person in the world whose approval he needed or cared about, Bobby was now committed to the truth, no matter what. Their other two buddies had fucked a whore, and Bobby had gone into the room and paid the same whore extra to not tell his friends that he had *not* fucked her. When the pimp's screaming had brought them into the room, Bobby and the others immediately realized that the much younger girl on the bed was not the whore who had been with them. They could only speculate that the whore who had fucked his buddies had refused a fourth customer, and the young pimp, not wanting to lose the revenue, had substituted his younger sister.

Preacher tried to process this new information. "They did see the girl move before we ran?"

Bobby hesitated, Preacher asked again, almost imploringly, "She did move?" Another hesitation. Bobby swiveled his head from his seat on the bed, making eye contact, and said, softly, "No." But then he added, "You couldn't have fucked the girl to death, that's crazy; you probably just popped her cherry."

Billy Ray was silent a while, then he said, slowly, "The problem, Bobby, is that I don't know what I did to the girl." More silence followed.

"So, my best friend has been a queer all our lives, and I didn't know it. I may have fucked a child, but I don't know. Hell, I may have killed her, but I don't know."

"You are the best man I've ever known," Bobby said. Billy Ray flashed Bobby a "don't fuck with me" look, then stood and pushed Bobby hard in the chest with both hands, slamming him against the wall.

"No, I'm not!" He hit Bobby with a right cross, then a left, another right and another left, losing count. Bobby, somehow defying survival instinct, never raised his hands in defense, just taking punches until his body slid down the wall into a sitting position, bleeding profusely from his nose, mouth, and cuts on his cheeks. Hazily, Bobby saw Billy Ray standing before him, saw him draw his gun.

"Do it. Kill me," Bobby said. But Preacher turned and walked away, police gun in hand.

Amazing Grace

Bobby, face cut and bruised, called in sick the next day, but Preacher had gone in to work. During the daily briefing Jarhead noticed his bruised knuckles, and Preacher noticed

Jarhead noticing. Jarhead was about to open his mouth when he was met with the "don't fuck with me" look, so intense that even Jarhead backed down.

It was a quiet Sunday morning, and the police radio was silent by two a.m. At home, Bobby, listening to the radio, heard Suzie-Q say, "And now I have a request from one of my friends in blue. Here's Emily Lou Harris and 'Amazing Grace.'"

Bobby's throat closed with fear. *"I never want to hear that song again, but do want it played at my funeral,"* Preacher had said. Bobby called the dispatcher, who called back a few minutes later to say Preacher wasn't answering the radio.

"Send a unit to the old boat ramp!" Bobby told the dispatcher, then threw on some clothes and frantically drove to their old fishing site, their old thinking place. He was filled with relief when from a distance he could see the uniform standing beside the car; but as he drew closer it became clear that the uniform was only an illusion of his friend.

Preacher had spent much of the night in his patrol car by the banks of the Chattahoochee, remembering that first year on the force and all that had happened since. He had called the radio station and asked Suzy-Q to play *that* song for him. As the song played, he had removed his gun belt, shoes, and uniform. Standing, nude, beside his patrol car, he neatly hung the uniform on a clothes hanger that was hanging from the glass in the car door. He placed his shoes on the ground beneath the trousers and his uniform hat on top of the car. He walked the short distance to his first love, the Chattahoochee, walked into her cool, welcoming waters, swam for a while, and then allowed her to wrap her swirling arms around him and take him wherever she wanted. Preacher had crossed the river.

Niner arrived only moments after Bobby, who grabbed Niner's walkie and screamed into it, "Nine-Thousand, Nine-Thousand, request river rescue ten-eighteen!" Niner knew that upon hearing the officer down call all units would come at break-neck speed to get to their brother-in-blue, endangering their own lives and the lives of others. Observing the scene at the boat ramp, Niner took the walkie from Bobby and told the dispatcher, "Slow them down, but send them on." Bobby's shoulders slumped, all hope gone.

They all arrived quickly—the new sergeant who had not

yet earned the nickname "Sarge," the Lieutenant, Jarhead, and I. B.'s replacement. They all stared at the ghostly looking uniform "standing" beside Preacher's patrol car. The veteran cops had seen it before; suicides would often clean their homes, bathe, and fold their clothes neatly before killing themselves.

The river rescue unit began its operation, but nobody thought Preacher would be found soon. The Chattahoochee is a devil in disguise: a slow, lazy flow of water on the surface, powerful currents beneath. But sooner or later she always coughed up her prey somewhere down river.

The detectives and crime scene units did their jobs. Preacher's patrol car was towed to headquarters for further processing. Only the lieutenant, the sergeant, and the rest of Preacher's squad remained. On Jarhead's arrival, seeing Bobby's face, he had asked, "What the hell happened to you? You look like you tried to sandpaper a bobcat's ass." But Bobby's expression and the situation convinced Jarhead to shut up. The squad had said little since.

Now, breaking the silence, Bobby said, "Why Billy Ray? He was the best of us." There were mumbled agreements, but Jarhead begged to differ.

"Bullshit, Floyd, Preacher was a wimp." Bobby lunged at him, stopped only by Niner's intervention and restraint. This time Jarhead wouldn't quiet, adding, "He was a fucking do-gooder, an i-dealist who wanted the world to be like the heaven he always talked about; a beautiful place where all God's children hold hands and sing Kumbaya. Well the world ain't like that, it's fucked up, and there ain't no happy endings."

This earned him the usual chorus telling him to fuck off. Jarhead walked away, giving them the finger. "Fuck *all* you girls!" he shouted. The lieutenant broke in then, saying that anybody who wanted to could take the rest of the night off and go home. Bobby, who was off duty already, went home to try to make sense of the senseless. Nobody else asked to go home; they all went back to their beats immediately, except for Jarhead.

The lieutenant saw Jarhead by the river, standing at water's edge, staring across to the other side. He walked down to where Jarhead stood.

"You OK, Jarhead?"

"I'm a little troubled, Loo."

The lieutenant, having never heard Jarhead express any emotion other than anger, replied sympathetically and inquisitively, "Yeah, what is it, Jar?"

Jarhead began, "You know how Preacher was always talking about how his daddy, the real preacher, used to preach that crossing the river was like crossing over to heaven?" The Lieutenant nodded. Jarhead, still staring across the Chattahoochee, hesitated a minute.

"Well," Jarhead confessed, "it troubles me that when I die all I have to look forward to is going to fucking Alabama!"

The Chattahoochee River looking from Georgia toward Alabama.

Author's Notes

I think many people who enjoy reading think about writing the next great American novel, or at least *a* novel. The core of the above story has been in my mind for over forty years, and it was to be my novel. Well, the years taught me that I had neither the talent nor the patience to write a novel. So my "novel" became the vignettes in this story.

All of my stories are fiction, but certainly some draw from personal experience. The story about riding with the fictional character, Niner, to the accidental shooting of a two-year-old is loosely based on truth. It was my first death call as a rookie cop. I am quite certain that I peered through a doorway and saw the bloodied body of the victim; but, if I did, my mind has never allowed me to "see" that image again. Repressing this kind of image was part of my training, and it would be filed away out of sight. I had known for more than two years that the scene would be included in "Crossing the River," but it was not until December 2015, thirty-nine years after the incident, that I finally wrote the story. As I wrote the last line—"And for Niner and Preacher, another unwanted memory, this one of blood and brains and a lifeless little body"—I found myself sobbing. Once I had regained my composure, I realized that I had not been crying for my own pain, I was doing something I had not done before: I was crying for that little girl. Sweetheart, I am so sorry it took me so long to grieve for you.

[II]
A Life Remembered

ATANASIO SHUFFLED ALONG ON NIKIS AVENUE IN Thessalonki, near the famous White Tower, the blue waters of the Aegean slapping against the sea wall to his right. He shuffled because his legs would no longer stretch to a normal walking stride. He was old. He was once six feet tall; now his back hunched, the spine curved forward. He had shrunk. His posture caused him to look downward. Just as well. Few people acknowledged him. Sometimes he felt invisible among the crowds on the streets. But he was still glad to be alive, for he had seen death.

Perhaps because he moved so slowly, the world around him seemed to move rapidly. Two young boys on skateboards were flying toward him. First hearing their approach, then raising his bent head to see them, he braced for impact, but the boys split left and right, going around the old man, laughing. *So fast*, he thought.

He slipped into memory. He and a friend were using sticks to guide old bicycle wheels along Egnatia Street in 1943. As they approached an intersection, a truck rounded the corner, then another, and another—many trucks. The trucks stopped and, as he and his friend gawked, soldiers piled out of the backs of the trucks, their leaders shouting orders in a language the boys could not understand. The Nazis had arrived in Thessaloniki.

The people had known they were coming. His parents had known they were coming, but they had told him not to worry. The Jews in the city may be in danger, but they were not Jewish. His parents were right, the Jews were in danger. The Nazis began rounding them up almost immediately.

The Nazis came to Atanasio's house at night, pounding on the door. When his father opened the door, the Nazis, led by an SS officer in a black uniform, pushed their way into the house, not waiting for an invitation. The officer told his father to call everyone into the parlor. His mother and his little sister descended the stairs and joined them. His father asked the officer why they were there. The Nazi looked at his father with…what? contempt, maybe, and said, *"Sie Juden sind!"* ("You are Jews!") His father and mother protested simultaneously, "No, we are not Jews, we are Orthodox!" The officer shouted, "Liars, your neighbor signed a document swearing that you are Jews!" His father and the neighbor were not friends. The neighbor had once failed to pay his father, a cobbler, for a pair of shoes. His father had taken the case to a magistrate, and the neighbor's reputation was damaged—but to do this? The Nazi ignored his parents' protests and pleas. As ordered, his parents hastily packed two suitcases, and he and his family were led away into the night. By the end of February 1943, almost all of the approximately 49,000 Jews of Thessaloniki had been deported, most to the Auschwitz-Birkenau camps in Poland.

A car horn startled him as he was about to step into the street against the crossing light, and he returned from remembrance to the present. His life in old age consisted of four primary activities: sleeping, eating, walking, and looking out his window. It was a solitary life. He was no longer a participant in life; he was an observer.

He sat at his window, peering into the park across the street from the old, rundown apartment building where he occupied a one-room apartment. The day was closing, darkness approaching. He saw them, a man and a woman, as he did every Wednesday evening. They embraced, as they always did, passionately; then the glances all around, did anyone see them who shouldn't? They sat on the park bench, a little conversation, some touching, and soon passionate kissing. Then they arose and left for whatever place they used for their secret rendezvous.

He remembered. They had worked together, he and his mistress. She was young and beautiful, and for reasons Atanasio never understood, she wanted him. Each time they met he swore to himself that it would be the last, but she always pulled him back. However, his mistress quickly tired of his sexual strangeness. The affair lasted only a few months, but his shame and guilt lasted a lifetime. He loved his wife. A deep breath of regret, and his mind returned to the present. He shuffled off to bed, guilt still flogging him.

Walking again, he saw a family being evicted from their apartment, their suitcases in hand. A man in a suit—

the landlord, he assumed—and a policeman close by. He remembered the Nazi, his mother and father carrying suitcases. His mother was crying, and his father seemed frightened, something he had never seen before. There were the others in the somber parade, mostly Jews, carrying suitcases for an unwanted journey to an unknown destination. At the railroad station they were herded onto freight cars like animals amidst the sounds of shouting Nazis and barking German shepherd dogs. The cars were filled with people until there was room only to stand or squat. The trip was horrible. The smell of urine and feces became unbearable as people shuffled between each other to use the one bucket in a corner of the car. An old man standing next to him slowly slid down the wall of the car to a squatting position, dead. Watching this then, he had not been sure what it meant to die, but now death would be his close companion. About four hours had elapsed between the time the Nazis knocked on the door of his home and the time the train left the station. In about four hours, his world had gone mad.

"Move along," the policeman monitoring the eviction said to him, startling him back from his memories. He walked. He stopped at a park bench for his lunch: some bread, a slice of meat, a piece of cheese. Raising food to mouth, he looked up, and his hand froze. Across the street he saw a homeless man, thin, gaunt, missing a leg, hand held out, begging. His mind again slipped into memory. He had never been as hungry as when the train had stopped. Where were they? What city? What country? *Conditions inside the train car were so horrible any place must surely be better*, he thought.

The car doors opened. The shouting in German and the barking of dogs resumed. People hurriedly climbed from the cars, some falling out, a long line of stinking humanity, thousands of them, formed alongside the train cars. Rumors spread rapidly. There would be a shower, thank God. It became clear that as the line moved forward the men were being separated from the women and children. More rumors were spread. Suddenly, his mother put her hand on his shoulder and whispered to him, "When the soldier asks you how old you are tell him you are fifteen." His parents had taught him that it was wrong to lie, so he replied, "But mother, that is a lie, I am only twelve." His mother grabbed the front of his shirt and pulled him forward until his face was only inches from hers, and with a fierceness in her eyes and voice that he had not known she possessed, she said, simply, "You will tell him!" He said he would. He had never in his short life been so frightened. The lie had saved his life. He and his father were forced into one line and his mother and little sister into another. He would never see his mother or sister again.

A police car sped past, blasting its siren; chasing away his memories. He again was aware of the homeless man across the street. He left the park bench, crossed the street, and offered the man his bread. A tear rolled down the beggar's cheek as he accepted the bread. Had the homeless man also known the hunger of Birkenau? Perhaps. He, too, was old. Offering no words to the homeless man, the old man shuffled away.

He roused slowly from a nap on the park bench, his head leaning forward and to one side, drooling. Opening his eyes, he saw shoes, his shoes. Not the ones on his feet, but shoes he had made. As a child Atanasio had marveled at his father's ability to transform a piece of cowhide into beautiful shoes. He remembered how his father would hold up the finished product, admiring the shoe as he would a work of art. They *were* art. His father taught him well, and his later work was almost as good as his father's. He loved shoes. His skill as a cobbler had given him a good life and a connection to his father. He hated shoes. His memory took him to the shoe room. He could see them, thousands of works of art, the pride of so many artists, piled high in that warehouse in Birkenau. Shoes without people. Works of art with no one to appreciate them. It was someone's job to collect the shoes. It was not his job. He would have thanked God for that, but God had abandoned the souls in Birkenau. The shoes moved. Not the shoes he saw in the pile at Birkenau—they were dead—the shoes next to him at the park bench. It brought him back from memory. He looked at the destitute drunk sitting next to him and wearing his creation, now scuffed and worn. *Just like me*, he thought.

He shuffled down the street. He stopped, staring at nothing. It happened sometimes. His mind became a kaleidoscope of memories, flashing rapid images of the past. The images so consumed his mind that he couldn't even process the neural message to put one foot forward. He was stuck. Sounding as if it were coming from the other end of a long tunnel, he heard a voice ask, "Are you OK?" The kaleidoscope slowed and then stopped. It was her! It was not her, but it was her eyes looking at him! *No, please, not her,* he thought. "Are you OK?" the girl's voice asked again. It was not the girl! He looked at the girl before him, attempted a smile, said, "Yes," and shuffled on, back in the reality of anonymity and invisibility that was now his life.

He sat at his window, watching children play in the park. His wife had wanted children. He was infertile, perhaps, the doctors said, due to the starvation he had suffered as an adolescent at Birkenau. His wife, he had thought, was a saint. She remained with him despite his inability to procreate and his sexual peculiarities. His "sexual peculiarities," that's what his wife had called it. Only now did it occur to him to wonder if she had sought satisfaction with someone else. Through thirty years of marriage he had never intentionally looked at his wife nude. If, by chance, she appeared before him nude, he turned away. He never touched her breasts or between her legs with his hands. He never looked in her eyes when they made love. She had asked, but he would offer no explanation for his behavior. Now, he fought the encroaching memory of the cause he could never forget nor express. The girl! *Please, stop looking at me*, he begged, knowing he had no right to ask that of her.

He left his window and lay on his bed, hoping the girl would leave and not return in his sleep. But he lay awake, and he remembered. He carried them. It was his job. It was what kept him alive in Birkenau. He was a Sonderkommando. His job was to carry them from the "showers" to the ovens.

He didn't put them in the ovens. He and his co-workers carried them on a litter to the crematorium and left long lines of bodies that would soon become smoke. He carried the feet end. They were all nude, their clothing already collected, their shoes in the dead shoe pile. Though he was at their feet, he never looked at their faces. That way, he reasoned, they were just bodies. Is a body without a face human, he wondered? He did not know until after liberation that his mother and little sister had "showered," been carried on litters, and become smoke within three hours of arriving at Birkenau.

He was fourteen that day. He had seen hundreds, or was

it thousands, of nude people: old men, women, children, all faceless bodies to him. Every day it was the same, until that day. He had never seen such a beautiful body. Her breasts were perfection. She lay there, one leg to the side, slightly exposing her. They put the litter down, rolled the body off, and his co-worker walked away mindlessly. Atanasio hesitated, and then knelt beside her. His hands moved seemingly without his mind's awareness. One hand was on her breast. His other hand touched her between her legs. A finger slipped inside her. *Oh God, she is warm inside!* he thought. His heart raced, he gasped. Could she be alive? Shocked, he did what he never did, he looked at her face. Her eyes were open! He fell backward, frightened, ashamed, a shame that would haunt him for the rest of his life, and be the worst of many painful memories. She was looking at him, but she was dead. It was a secret he could not share, not even with his wife of thirty years, who he could not touch or even look at intimately. It was that secret, that memory that consumed his mind as he fell asleep.

When he looked into a mirror he did not recognize the old man looking back at him. Could he be that old? He felt the ravages of age, the discomfort, the inflexibility. He changed socks only weekly, not due to a shortage of socks, but because of the difficulty and pain of bending his back far enough to change them. His tiny apartment had no shower, only a bath tub. It had been years since he could use that, bathing instead while standing at the sink. Yes, he was aware of all these physical difficulties of age, but his image in the mirror always shocked him. Sometimes, while walking, he would stare at the wall of one of the old buildings he knew from childhood, and he would see himself as if he were looking into a mirror, but he didn't see the old man with whom the mirror punished him. The young image of himself he saw in the wall always made him smile.

He shuffled past a cemetery. A burial was in progress, and Atanasio thought of his wife. He hoped she was at peace, but he would not say "God rest her soul," because he did not believe in a God concerned with the peace of the human soul. An omnipotent God with the power to interfere in the affairs of humans yet still allow wars, famine, disease—and, yes, Birkenau—would be an evil God not worthy of worship or even belief. His wife believed. Her priests had tried to console him at her death, had told him he must not question the will of God because mere mortals cannot understand His mind. He had told the priests that if God had used His mind to decide that his wife should suffer the slow, painful death by cancer she had endured, and had decided that millions should die in the Holocaust, then damn God! "Blasphemy!" the priests had retorted.

He sat on the park bench. The sun was warm; a light breeze rustled leaves. He breathed in the crisp fall air with slow, shallow breaths; slower, then slower still, until there was no breath. He had no family. His father, like his mother and sister, had become smoke at Birkenau, never again to be seen except perhaps in a passing cloud, or so he liked to think. He had no friends. The government would take whatever money was found in his apartment and bury him in a pauper's grave. There would be no funeral, as he had offended the priests, and there would be no marker.

Author's Notes

A few years ago I came face-to-face with dying in a way I had never experienced. I was the primary care-giver for my mother in the last year of her life. I had promised her that I would take care of her at home as long as possible. I did the best I could (though one always wonders if one does good enough) as her body and mind deteriorated. Momma did not know who I was the last six months. One day I awoke, and she did not; hers then a life once lived. She was ninety-one. I had thought that I was helping Momma live. The hospice nurse told me I was helping her die. It was the hardest thing I have ever done. It darkened my soul, and the light has yet to fully return.

During my travels in Europe in 2014, I had seen elderly people in every city I visited, but no story related to aging formed in my mind until I was in Thessaloniki, Greece. I had just visited a Holocaust museum in the city and, as I walked along a street next to the Aegean Sea, I stopped in a small shop. The first thing I noticed was a postcard with a photo of an elderly Greek man and woman walking along a street.

I bought the card and a story began to form. I first put pen to paper for this story on the train leaving Thessaloniki.

[III]

Searching for Eva

KAROL WOULD OFTEN SIT ON THE CHARLES BRIDGE, NOT really looking for her, for she no longer lived in Prague, but remembering the day they met there and the daily walks they took across the bridge, lingering and marveling at the beautiful statues, the buildings of the old city, and the boats traversing the Vltava River. He was a distinguished professor of sociology at Charles University in Prague, one of the oldest universities in Eastern Europe, but he had written some controversial commentaries on freedom. He had argued for minimal state prohibition of human behavior. Most controversial were his thoughts on sexual freedom. He had argued that government prohibition of any consensual sexual act was an abuse of the state's power. That had angered the conservatives and the religionists, papists and Protestants alike. Karol was a-theist, though not a-god-ist, but the fools didn't know the difference.

It was his defense of sexual freedom that was most responsible for his loneliness. He exercised none of the kind of sexual freedom he professed, until Eva left. He had been a devoted and faithful husband and a good father. His wife had not left him because of any sexual indiscretions on his part—there were none. A Lutheran, she did not personally approve of his academic ideas, but the public attacks against her husband, and the embarrassment it caused her, drove her to abandon him and to remove his daughter from his life. Loneliness, sadness…must the truth cost so much, he often wondered. He had loved Eva deeply, the only love of his life. He did not understand that she simply did not have the strength of conviction his academic mind had given him. Her departure from Karol's life—and it was complete, save for the annual photo of their daughter she would send to him with no message—left a hole in his heart that was never to be filled. He remained celibate for two years after she left him.

The trees had lost their leaves, the days had shortened, it had gotten colder, and his loneliness had worsened as it always did as winter approached. The cabaret was just off Wenceslaus Square, in the center of Prague. Karol had walked past it many times, always waving off the woman on the sidewalk who invited him to go inside. He walked under the neon sign. The woman invited him inside as she had a hundred times before. He raised his hand to wave her off, but then almost stumbled as he abruptly stopped. The woman, who recognized him, was startled that he had stopped but recovered quickly and said, "Good evening." He replied, "What is this place?" He immediately felt foolish, standing under the neon cabaret sign fully aware, as is everyone in Prague, that many such places are brothels. The woman answered, "It's a gentlemen's club." He just stood there until she said once again, "Would you like to come inside?" Surprising himself, he answered, "May I have a tour?"

He followed her inside. What he saw inside seemed a manifestation of his teachings on sexual freedom. Beautiful women, nude from the waist up, wearing only a white towel wrapped around their waists. Some lounged alone, some sat on a lounger with a man, some were seated at a bar, others were in a Jacuzzi, and one sat behind the foggy glass wall of a sauna, completely nude! All were seemingly unaware that their breasts were exposed as they conversed with each other or with men, who all wore white bath robes. The entire room was black and white—white towels, black and white sofas and loungers, glass tables. *What a clean room,* Karol thought.

He asked, awkwardly, "What happens here?" His pretty guide answered directly and concisely, "It costs 2,000 korunas to enter, and you may stay for twelve hours." She told him the entry fee included the Jacuzzi, sauna, non-alcoholic drinks, buffet food, and conversation with any of the "girls" on the loungers, at the bar, in the Jacuzzi or in the sauna. She then added that a private session with any girl could be had for thirty minutes for 700 korunas or one hour for 1,300 korunas.

"What is a private session?"

She again replied matter-of-factly, "That is full-service sex, anything you want."

A beautiful girl seated at the bar smiled at him, stood, and removed the towel wrapped around her waist to expose tiny red bikini panties and what he thought must have been a near perfect body. Karol's senses were heightened and he was drowning in thoughts and emotions. He said, simply, "I must go."

Karol went back the next night. The woman on the street smiled when she saw him stop beside her. He paid the 2,000 korunas, placed his clothes in a locker, donned the white robe, and stepped back into the heaven he had seen the night before.

Or was it hell? It was prostitution. He had lectured on prostitution in his sociology classes at Charles University. He abhorred the world of drug addiction, human trafficking, and the sex slavery of forced prostitution. However, he had lectured that in a free society that valued gender equity, women could not be denied the right to choose to seek their own survival through prostitution, a position, perhaps surprisingly, agreed with by some liberal feminists.

He had asked his students if there was any difference

between a prostitute who has sex with a man she does not love so that she can pay her bills, and a wife who no longer loves her husband but continues to have sex with him so he will pay her bills. Or, what of a husband who no longer loves his wife but remains in the marriage and having sex because he does not want to lose half of his money in a divorce? Is he not prostituting himself for money? And what of young women who only date and have sex with men so the men will buy them expensive gifts, take them for rides in Lamborghinis or on yachts, and on vacations to exotic places. Is not the prostitute who chooses to work in a brothel simply a more honest prostitute than the others?

As he stood in the black and white room he realized that nothing that happened there was black-and-white. He walked awkwardly through the room, smiling shyly back at the girls who smiled at him, not all did. What was he looking for? Karol tried not to admit it to himself, but he was looking for a girl who reminded him of his Eva.

He saw her. She did not look like Eva, but the similarity was there. She was seated at the bar. He approached the empty seat next to her and just stood there. She smiled and asked if he would like to sit. He did. They exchanged names. He said, awkwardly, "I don't know what to do." She laughed and replied, "What do you want to do?" His eyes shifted from her eyes to her bare breasts. She uncrossed her legs and the white towel separated exposing her legs and the fact that she wore black panties. He had seen other men touching the girls they were sitting with, still, he asked shyly, "Can I touch you?" She again laughed, a friendly laugh, and replied, "Of course." He touched her warm, smooth thigh, while looking at her breasts. His heart rate jumped. He had not touched a woman in two years.

He didn't know where the courage came from, if that's what it was, but he said, "The lady said I can pay for a private session." He did. The room was large, the size of a normal bedroom, and clean. There was a king-size mattress on the floor covered by a red sheet. The dim lighting in the room and the red sheet gave the room an exotic ambiance. He scanned the room until his eyes met the girl's eyes. She let the white towel drop from her waist, the black panties were gone, and she was completely nude. He gasped and his heart beat raced.

The girl walked past him into a shower room, leaving

the door open, and began to bathe. She called out to him, "Don't you want to shower? Join me, there's room." He did. She faced him, took his already erect penis in her hand and washed it as he gasped for breath. She smiled, turned her back to him, raised onto her toes, stepped back, and settled down onto his erection, her perfectly round ass soft but firm against him. She reached between her legs and stroked him. "God!" He reached around her and gently caressed her breasts. They stood there a moment, the warm water raining down upon them until she said, "Are you ready?" He was.

She dried him and then herself. She took his hand and walked him to the mattress. She nudged him and he lay down. She kneeled down next to him and grasped his erection. His entire body stiffened and he said, "Wait, lie down beside me and talk with me." She did. She was, she said, a university student, but not at Charles. She denied that drug addiction, alcoholism or coercion played any part in her decision to be a prostitute. She said she needed money for tuition and could not make enough at the other jobs she had tried. He doubted her, and told her so. She assured him that more than half the girls working there were students. Perhaps, he thought.

He then said something that she had never heard before, "I have paid for one hour of your time. You need not perform any sex act. You may simply lie here next to me and talk for the next hour." She was genuinely confused and said, "But you paid." He replied, "I have paid for your time. You are free to choose to not perform any sex act." This, Karol believed, allowed him to honor his teachings. She thought for a moment and said, "You have paid, I must do something; what do you want?" Was it shock, confusion, principle, work ethic? He did not know her motivation. But he knew what he wanted.

Despite her religious upbringing, Eva had been very comfortable with her sexuality, more so even than he. In fact, she was the aggressor in their very good sexual relationship. Foreplay varied, but it always ended the same. She would push him down onto his back, straddle him, and say, "Now I will fuck you slowly until we come." That was Eva in bed.

He told the girl how he wanted her. She straddled him and rocked back and forth slowly. It had been so long since he had felt the inside of a woman that he came quickly. The physical feelings of orgasm were wonderful, but the girl didn't feel like Eva inside. She did resemble Eva, that's why he had chosen her, but she was not Eva. Overall, he found the experience lacking. For several days he contemplated the experience. The nice lady who had given him the initial tour had said that they would do almost anything to please their clients. He knew what he wanted.

The first girl had been pretty and resembled Eva but he found that as he looked at her she was distracting, because she was not Eva. He decided that what he needed was a girl who *felt* like Eva. He could then simply close his eyes and imagine that it was Eva, he reasoned; admitting to himself that he may have lost the ability to reason. The friendly lady at the club listened to his request and quickly agreed to help. Henceforth, he would be blindfolded and lying on the mattress in a completely darkened room before the girl arrived. He would never see the girl, and she would never see him. She would be instructed to say nothing, just push him from his seated position back onto the bed, straddle him, and rock slowly back and forth until he came. He would imagine Eva.

So the search began, a different girl every time. And so it was for seven years. Then, on a day like all the others, a girl sat upon him and it was a miracle, he thought. Her legs were the same as Eva's. She felt exactly like Eva's insides, and she rocked back and forth with the same perfect rhythm Eva had always used. She *was* Eva, but only in his mind.

He had been visiting "Eva" once a week, sometimes twice, for almost a year. He would simply ask the lady to send "Eva" to the dark room. He was back again; he needed "Eva." He was placed in the room, put on the black mask to shut out the small amount of light that entered the room from the street lights, aroused himself, and waited. He heard the door open and close. "Eva" kneeled next to him, stroked him gently to ensure he was erect, and straddled him. Immediately he wondered if her legs felt smaller. She took his erection in hand and guided it inside her, a little clumsily he thought. He saw his Eva in his mind as the girl began rocking back and forth. Wait, he thought! The rhythm of her rocking was off, and she was tighter around his erection. This is not "Eva"! He simultaneously snatched the mask from his eyes and turned on the light by the bed. He gasped! He had not seen her in person in eight years. Startled by his actions, recognition took Anna longer, as she only knew him from old photos. Then, her hand over her gaping mouth, she ripped herself from his erection and fled the room. He retched. Then he vomited. He too then fled the scene.

The girl he had called "Eva" had been sick that day and the new girl had been sent to the dark room. Her mother, Eva, had tried to keep her father's controversial ideas from Anna; indeed, had forbidden her from reading his work. But she was eighteen now and in university. She had read her estranged father's thoughts on freedom, which had enraptured her. She didn't need the money, her mother had a good income, and her father, despite Eva's refusal to allow him any contact with his daughter, never failed to make a generous monthly support payment. Anna had embraced radical feminism. Her body was hers, she reasoned; she would show the world, and herself, that she would do with her body as she pleased—this was a human right, she believed, as her father had taught.

Anna and her father would never speak of that horrible day. He shot himself in his office the next day. The bullet traveled right to left through his brain, bringing instant death. He had chosen what he once suggested in his lectures might be the ultimate act of human freedom, suicide. The note he left had said, "It is all my fault. No one has guilt but me. Must freedom cost so much?" Eva thought the note was for her.

Author's Notes

The inspiration for this story came from the photograph of a man sitting and gazing across the Charles Bridge in Prague, Czech Republic; which I bought from a street vendor on the bridge. I was intrigued by the photo. What was the man thinking? Was he looking for someone? I spent most of my time in Prague in the Old City, where I saw Charles University, founded in 1348, one of the oldest universities in Europe in continuous operation. It was not until my last night in Prague that I wandered away from the oldest part of the city to a newer, albeit still old, area. I had stumbled onto Wenceslas Square, the heart of the city, alive with activity. It was there that I saw several cabarets. It appeared to me that the cabarets were as much a part of the city as its beautiful buildings and human energy. It dawned on me that the citizens of Prague, including university professors, walked by these places every day and likely paid them little attention; just as our protagonist had until Eva left him. This story raises questions about the difference between abiding love and obsession.

[IV]

A Just Vengeance

GABRIEL AWOKE EARLY, KISSED HIS WIFE, AND SAID goodbye, receiving a sleepy reply, "I love you." Stealthily, to avoid waking her, he brushed his daughter's hair from her forehead, gently kissed her there, and left the two loves of his life. He was, his colleagues and friends would attest, the happiest man they knew.

It was eleven o'clock. He had just completed the morning surgery and exited the operating room. He saw the nurse first; she could not hold back her tears, despite years of delivering bad news. The hospital chaplain was standing beside the nurse. *Oh no*, he thought, *a patient must have died.* Then he saw the man and woman, badges dangling from chains around their necks.

The detectives told him what had happened. A strange silence enveloped him for a moment before his knees buckled and he fell forward at the waist, his head hitting the floor with a loud crack as he let out a scream surely heard throughout the entire hospital.

The brothers had been released on parole, again, for "good behavior," despite long records for drug convictions, burglaries, and minor assaults. In truth, they had *not* been released for good behavior; rather, the governor had given the parole board a new mission to control the prison population by releasing more inmates. The only other alternative was to raise taxes to build more prisons; and to raise taxes jeopardized the popularity of the governor, who makes appointments to the parole board. His wife and daughter had died to protect the jobs of politicians.

Since their release, the brothers had done well, by some parolee standards. They had been out seventy-five days and had reported to their parole officer the first Monday of each of their first two months of release; and they had passed the required drug tests. The day after their second report to the parole office they partied with old friends, and for the next two weeks had used methamphetamines repeatedly. To get money for more drugs, they began burglarizing homes—always during daytime, so nobody would be at home. On the day of the murders they had taken the last of their crank and had not slept in days. Before they left Gabriel's house, they set it on fire.

Perhaps due to the fire, the brothers left little physical

evidence at the scene other than DNA, but that was enough. A year later a jury found them both guilty of two counts of malice murder; and, because the state did not have the death penalty, they were both sentenced to life without parole. Perhaps because of the Hippocratic Oath, or perhaps because he was a Catholic, Gabriel had never supported the death penalty. He knew the verse in Romans: "Vengeance is mine, saith the Lord." Still, he admitted to himself, his priest, and God that he wished the brothers dead. Some years later, he heard that one of the brothers had been killed in prison. He was glad.

It had been thirty years since the murders when the prosecutor called and said, "We have a problem." In another, unrelated case it had been discovered that the state's forensic scientist had lied about the DNA results. All cases handled by that scientist, including that of Gabriel's wife and daughter, were reviewed. In cases where there was sufficient evidence of guilt beyond the DNA evidence, the convictions had been affirmed. However, in any case where DNA was the only evidence sufficient for conviction, the conviction was vacated and the offender was ordered released. Gabriel knew what this meant, but he asked anyway, "What are you saying?"

"I'm saying," the prosecutor replied, "that the man who killed your wife and daughter has been released."

Gabriel was sixty years old now. He had never remarried. The fire-damaged house that had been his family's home had been sold, as he could no longer live there. He had considered retiring, but his practice was all he had. His wife and child were dead. There was no other purpose in his life. Until now.

Gabriel had known at the time of the murders that his wife and daughter had both been violated. Thirty years earlier he had not wanted to know the details of their deaths. For some reason, the fact that one of the animals who had murdered them was free had changed that, and he wanted to know exactly how they had died. One of the detectives from that terrible day at the hospital had kept in touch with him, calling periodically just to talk. Gabriel dialed his number. The detective, who was now retired, tried unsuccessfully to dissuade him, but Gabriel persisted. The detective eventually agreed to get Gabriel the police report, but only if he read it in the detective's presence.

And so, with tears and a sickened stomach, he read the

report of the murders of his wife and daughter for the first time. The brothers had entered the house by breaking a glass pane in the back door. The bedrooms were upstairs, so the victims did not hear the breaking glass. While no one could be sure, it was almost certain that his wife was asleep when the animals entered the bedroom—there was no sign of struggle other than on the bed. Detectives speculated that his wife's struggle had awakened his daughter, and she had come to her mother's bedroom, as there was no evidence the brothers had ever entered his daughter's bedroom.

A broken jaw indicated that his wife had initially resisted her attackers. DNA showed that both men had sodomized her orally and raped her. She had then been turned onto her stomach and her hands and feet tied to bed posts. His twelve-year-old daughter was raped by one of the brothers, and she too had then been tied to the bed posts, also lying on her stomach. DNA also showed that mother and daughter were anally raped. The mother and daughter had been placed side-by-side on the king-size bed, where they would have been able to see the terror in each other's eyes. But the terror of rape would not have been the worst thing they saw. The brothers had found a gas can in the garage, doused the mother and daughter with it, and set them on fire. The last thing the loves of his life saw in each other's eyes was the unimaginable pain of burning alive.

Gabriel now had a purpose. He would dedicate his every waking moment to finding the animal who had taken love from him. He became, he admitted to himself, an animal stalking an animal. After finding the murderer, he began stalking him, not out of uncertainty or reluctance, but out of curiosity about the animal's life. He observed the animal go to work as a dishwasher at a restaurant; to bars where he smiled, drank, and laughed with others; and to whorehouses. One night, Gabriel followed him to a sex shop, where the rapist bought a magazine featuring domination and simulated rape.

It was the magazine that decided him. He followed the animal to his dingy lair, approaching him as he unlocked the door. The conversation was short.

"What do you want?" the rapist demanded, suspicious.

"You took my wife and daughter."

"Right, the doctor," the criminal sneered. Then, with a threatening tone, "Leave me alone."

"You shouldn't be free," Gabriel replied.

"Fuck you," said the animal. "I lost thirty years of my life in that hell-hole of a prison, and my brother died there."

"You should have been executed," Gabriel said, almost without emotion. The animal gave him an ugly smile and turned as if to enter his apartment, but then stopped. He turned back toward Gabriel and said, "You know what kept me alive in prison? It was your little girl's tight pussy as I fucked her again and again in my mind every night for thirty years."

Gabriel was left-handed, so the lightning-fast move of his hand caught the rapist off-guard. The razor-sharp scalpel slit his right carotid artery, and he gasped, eyes wide, as blood spurted from the artery. Death was quick—a blessing the animal didn't deserve, Gabriel thought. He went home and called the police, told the dispatcher he had committed murder, giving her the animal's address and telling her where police could find him.

He sat in his walnut-paneled study, expensive Persian rugs on the floor, beautiful antiques all about, and surrounded by bookcases filled with knowledge; the place his wife had called his "Shiloh," meaning "place of peace." Gabriel no longer believed in the God of his religion, the one who had killed his loves or allowed them to be killed. But he believed in the miracle of life, and, perhaps only because it was too painful to imagine otherwise, he believed there was a reunion of spirits after death. *I'm coming, my darlings*, he thought, as the needle found the vein and he pushed the Propofol into his arm.

Author's Notes

The idea for this story arose in Warsaw, Poland, in the summer of 2015, but I have no idea why Warsaw evoked it. At least three things influenced my thoughts: first, my experiences as a parole officer; second, the real murder of a Connecticut doctor's wife and two daughters by two men in the recent past; and lastly an old case in which a man's child was kidnapped, molested, and murdered. In that case the defendant, who was unquestionably guilty, was not convicted due to a technicality. Upon leaving the courthouse, he was killed by the child's distraught father. Although the father was clearly guilty of murder, no jury would convict him. Jurors chose to believe that the father's act was a just vengeance.

[V]

Forgiveness

IT WAS A SIN. DOMOKOS KNEW IT WAS A SIN. THE PRIESTS had told him since he was a small child. The Book said it was a sin, or at least the priests said the Book said it was. His mother and father had told him to trust the priests. If the Book was the word of God, as all those in his life seemed to believe, then God Himself said it was a sin.

For his entire life he had attended Saint Michael's Church, a short walk from the Danube in Budapest, and he was a believer. Every Sunday the congregation and he would recite the Prayer to Saint Michael:

> Saint Michael, the Archangel, defend us in battle.
>
> Be our defense against the wickedness and snares
>
> of the Devil. May God rebuke him, we humbly pray.
>
> And you, Prince of the heavenly host, by the power of God,
>
> thrust into Hell Satan and the other evil spirits
>
> who prowl the world for the ruin of souls.
>
> Amen.

He would always recite with extra emphasis the words, "Be our defense against the wickedness and snares of the Devil," and silently ask God for help with his own wicked ways. Still, he did it, had been doing it since that day as an adolescent when it first happened. No one had told him what would happen. He thought something was wrong with it. The priests had told him that it was a sin to touch it other than to urinate and to bathe.

It happened, that first time, when Domokos broke the rules, which he rarely did. He had heard other boys talk of sneaking behind the convent and climbing the fire escape to the roof, from which one could see the whole city spreading all around. He had climbed three stories when he caught a glimpse of movement through a window. He pressed against the wall beside the window, praying he had not been seen. A few moments passed, and he was confident that he had not been discovered. He had to cross in front of the window to continue to the roof, so he carefully peeked in to make sure no one was there. The nun's back was to him; she was naked from the waist up. He stared at her back for a moment before he realized she was standing in front of a mirror; and then his gaze shifted to the mirror. Her eyes were closed. He looked further down and saw that her hands were slowly moving across her breasts. His erection was instant—and he thought he might burst! He was unaware of his hand entering his pants, but there it was, touching his erection. He barely moved his hand, and only twice, before he felt a powerful surge from deep inside as he closed his eyes in ecstasy and tried to muffle a guttural sound of relief. His hand was wet, from what he didn't know. When his eyes opened he saw the nun still facing the mirror, but her eyes open and staring at his image in the mirror. Mortified at what he had done and—so much worse!—being discovered, Domokos fled down the fire escape as fast as he could and ran to his room, where he locked the door, as if that might protect him from the horrible punishment certain to come.

The next day at school, the nun stopped him in the hallway. He looked at the floor, his heart pounding harder than it had the day before. "Have you been to confession?" she asked. He shook his head. "Perhaps you should," she replied and walked away. He would attend that school for seven more years, and in all that time would never again make eye contact with that nun.

He did go to confession, however, and confessed to touching himself for pleasure, rather than just for pissing. He left out the part about the nun. Surely nobody told the priests everything, he rationalized. The priest had explained, as he had understood it as a boy, that in the beginning, just after God had created Adam and Eve in the Garden of Eden, it was not forbidden to touch it, even Eve could touch it. He imagined, only for a moment, the nun touching him. The priest continued, God had made the touching between Adam and Eve pleasurable, but only if they didn't eat the fruit of a particular tree. But when Adam succumbed to Eve's temptation to taste the forbidden fruit, God decreed that touching for pleasure was forever after a sin. *A fucking apple?* he thought. He didn't even know what "fucking" meant but had heard other boys saying it as an expression of emphasis or disbelief, and he was having trouble believing the story.

He did believe he had sinned. He had confessed, mostly, and had been given absolution. End of story. Except that he touched himself every day, sometimes more than once a day, for the rest of his life. He tried to stop. He didn't want to be a sinner. He didn't want to go to hell. Surely other boys did it; he couldn't be the only one.

He had thought it would stop after he grew older and married. His wife, also a devout Catholic, was young and very desirable. She, too, had heard the priest's warnings about the sin of sexual self-pleasure. But the work of the nuns had made, for her, sexual pleasure of any kind a sin; the ecstasy of orgasm so vile an act as to be avoided always. But she, too, had sinned. She had, in puberty, realized a desire, stronger than anything she had felt before, to touch herself—surely the Devil at work! But she had succumbed, and she had come. Mortified at her sin, she too had gone to confession.

She confessed to the priest that she had touched herself and waited silently for absolution, but absolution did not come so easily. The priest told her that to receive forgiveness for this terrible sin she must, before God, and him, confess completely. She must, the priest said, describe every sinful, pleasurable feeling from her first touch of herself. She did, and felt as if she were sinning again, as her words left her aroused. Reaching the climax of her confession, describing the orgasm, she heard the priest making muffled grunting sounds that concluded with a groan. She thought that she had so disgusted the priest with her sinful act that she had physically sickened him. She never touched herself there again.

He was wrong to think that marriage would end his desire to masturbate. Their wedding night grieved him still. She tolerated him, as the Church had taught she must, but only for the purpose of procreation. She immediately suppressed any feelings of pleasure, determined not to participate in any sinful act of pleasurable sex. For her, that first time and every time thereafter, sex was a physical act lacking any intimacy. Domokos was allowed to have her once a month, following her period, which she saw as proof of her failure to add to God's flock. He returned to pleasuring himself daily the day after their disastrous wedding night.

The years passed. No conception. Finally, the doctors told her it was not to be. She knew why. Despite what the doctors said, she was certain it was God's punishment for her so enjoying the sinful pleasure of orgasm when she was a child. The priest told her that God, in his infinite wisdom, was not punishing her but was instead protecting her from her weakness. While even the priests told her it would not be a sin to continue monthly sex with her husband for the purpose of procreation, after all the doctors are mere mortals and God can work miracles, she never again allowed him to touch her. He pleasured himself daily, remaining faithful to her, as God commanded, until she died. He was seventy when she died, and he was still blessed—or was it cursed?—with a strong libido and a cooperative organ.

He knew about them. Everybody knew about them. It was Budapest. There were some on *Vaci utca*, the same street as St. Michael's. Sometimes the girls would approach a man, handing out fliers, soliciting business. In name, they were massage parlors, and some were, but others were brothels. It was not long after his wife died that, while walking, he passed a sign reading "Massage, Plus." *Plus what?* he thought. He stopped, turned around, walked down the stairs to a basement door and went inside. Had the Devil possessed him? He so longed for human touch, for a woman's touch. Was God testing him? Could he be as strong as Job? Could any man? Why had God created men with such a strong desire, and then denied them the right to satisfy that desire? *That fucking apple!*

It was a sin. He knew it was a sin. He gave the woman the

money she requested for her to touch him. He entered a dimly lit room. As instructed, he removed his clothes, showered, and lay down on the mattress on the floor, a towel across him. He was stunned when she, standing over him, removed all her clothes. He had not seen a naked woman since his wedding night so many years ago when his wife, at his insistence, for the first and last time, allowed him to look at her before darkening the room to consummate the marriage.

The woman smiled at him. He was embarrassed, both by his aged body and by the towel raised by his erection. She moistened her hands with massage oil, kneeled beside him, and began gently rubbing his shoulders, then his breasts. *My God*, he thought! No woman had ever touched his breasts. She massaged his stomach with oil, then, still on her knees, she spread her legs, lifting one across his body…he could see her shaved vagina! She sat on him, facing him, he looking up at her eyes, then down…her breasts…her belly…to her no longer secret place that spread over his legs. Then she touched him…there! Domokos gasped, then, embarrassingly, whimpered like a baby; and tears rolled from his eyes as she slid her hand up and down. Three times down, three times up and he exploded with an ecstasy he had never experienced from the touch of his own hand.

He expected God to strike him dead. He would deserve it. He had sinned. But he didn't care! *If the pleasure he had just experienced was such a sin*, he thought, *perhaps his punishment might be to experience that feeling eternally in hell.* An evil thought that he regretted immediately.

As he regained his senses, the woman cleaned him and herself. Not knowing what to do next, he began to rise. She motioned him to lie back, and he did. She covered him with a towel. "We have time," she said, and then she lay next to him, wiped the remaining tears from his eyes, and put her head on his chest. She was cuddling him. He had never been cuddled. This was sin?

Of course it was sin. He had been taught that it was, and he never really doubted that. Yet he continued to sin, and in new ways! He was introduced to "sliding." This particular sin called for a girl, and there were different girls over the years, to oil her body and then, lying on top of him, slide her oily breasts, stomach and closed legs over his erection until he came. And there was the four-hand massage. Two girls!

There will be a special place in hell for me, he fretted. He did not *want* to go to hell. He attended mass at St. Michael's every Sunday because he believed in and sincerely worshipped the majesty and wonder of God. He confessed his sins and asked for forgiveness, but he kept sinning. In his seventy-fifth year, after five years of the sin of masturbation with many different women, the most beautiful girl he had ever seen lay beside him, looking into his eyes, smiling, her breasts lying on his chest, her hand gently stroking him, when his penis and his heart both exploded at the same time. "God, forgive me!" he shouted, asking for the final time.

Author's Notes

In Budapest, Hungary, there are many old churches and cathedrals; many of which I visited, including Saint Michael's Church, which was originally the property of the Dominicans (the Blackfriars). First established in about 1240, the church was destroyed and rebuilt several times.

Also in Budapest there are many massage parlors. Just a short distance from my hotel I noticed a sign adorned with a photo of a beautiful girl and the words, "Massage and more…" I should note that my hotel was not in a seedy part of the city; it was one block from the Danube River in a very nice tourist shopping and dining area, and only a few blocks from St. Michael's.

When I walked into Saint Michael's for the first time I picked up a pamphlet that included the Prayer to St. Michael. The inspiration for this story came from the prayer, particularly the line, "Be our defense against the wickedness and snares of the Devil."

[VI]

The Alley

HE STOOD IN THE dim, narrow alley peering into the window. Earlier that day he had arrived in Amsterdam by train. Upon exiting Central Station he had stood staring at the building's perfectly balanced twin towers and gold-tinged carvings, in awe that something so utilitarian could be so beautiful. He had toured Amsterdam that day, the Rijksmuseum, Van Gogh, Rembrandt, the tree-lined canals...beautiful! Mary would have loved it.

He and Mary had met at 18. It was a passionate meeting, and despite the odds, the passion never died, at least not until Mary did. "God took her when she was just 60, the bastard," he had spat. God didn't just take her; he tortured her with a slow cancer that gradually disintegrated her. He had suffered a terrible, helpless pain as his Mary slowly and painfully disappeared, and his happiness ended.

The clang of a distant tram brought him back to the alley in which he now stood, and to the girl in the window underneath the red light. She was beautiful, tanned, perfectly proportioned, smiling, and wearing a black bikini. Black lingerie, his weakness, and Mary had known it. She would surprise him at times, appearing in the doorway wearing only bra and panties, one arm stretched upward along the doorframe, the other propped on a protruding hip, and on her face that universally understood expression that said, "Fuck me."

The girl opened the door next to the window, startling him back to the present. "Hi, I'm Isabella." Her English had a heavy Russian accent. He tried to maintain eye contact, but his eyes wandered down...her breasts...her belly...to that place men so crave to be. She reached out and took his hand, and he was instantly aroused. Oddly, it was not her beautiful face or body that aroused him, but the touch of her hand.

She gently pulled him toward her and led him inside the

room with the window. As she closed the red curtains, she quoted an amount he didn't really hear. Mindlessly, he took from his pocket a wad of bills, not even knowing how much the Dutch currency was worth, and offered it to her. She took some and placed it on a table, returning the remainder to him. Then, in her broken English, she suggested he remove his clothes. Unable to make eye contact with her or even to move, he simply looked down in silence.

It had been five years since Mary was so cruelly taken from him. Truth be told (and he would never tell it), he had never been with another woman. He had had dinner with a few women since Mary died, and his libido was strong, but thoughts of sex with another woman always felt like betrayal. This is how he had found himself in Amsterdam: maybe if it was not intimate, it wouldn't feel like betrayal.

"What?" he said. The Russian had said something. "You are shy, so cute." She removed his shirt, then reached down, unbuckled his belt, and removed his pants and underpants, he offering unthinking assistance. He stood there, like a frightened little boy, staring at the floor, naked. She removed her bra and tiny panties—black, he registered again. Was it the hand of providence or of the Devil himself? Both now naked, she took his hand and led him to the bed, where she gently pushed him down. He lay there, his entire body as stiff as his erection.

The girl kneeled beside him on the bed as he stared at the ceiling. She said, "It's OK, I do for you." She straddled him, taking him into her hand and guiding him inside her. He looked into her eyes for the first time since the window in the alley. He gasped as he slid inside her soft, warm, wet place, feeling as if he could be returning to the warmth and safety of his mother's womb. His heart raced as she slowly rocked back and forth, back and forth, until he repeatedly called out, "Oh God, Oh God!" as climax neared—though he no longer believed God was present. As he burst into orgasm his body and mind emptied of all pain, and he momentarily left his lonely world.

With the orgasm he had shouted, "Ah," and his eyes had opened. But then he was confused. He looked around and saw the familiar walls of his hotel room. It was not the woman but his own hand that was wrapped around his now softening erection; his ejaculate was not inside the beautiful Russian but had soiled his own stomach.

"Oh," he remembered aloud. The Russian girl had opened the door, smiled at him, and told him her name. "Hi, Isabella," he had said, then walked away. As his breathing slowed now, his eyes moistened, and he said to no one, "Oh, Mary, I'm so sorry."

Author's Notes

This story was written during my visit to Amsterdam in July of 2014. The inspiration for the story was the confluence of two observations. As I walked the streets I noticed a large number of older people walking alone, particularly men. Then I visited the famous red light district which is listed in the city's tourism brochure as one of the top tourist attractions.

I sat at one of Amsterdam's many outdoor cafes, under the shade of trees and beside a canal, thinking about the older men I had seen walking alone. I wrote the story within an hour while sipping on a cappuccino. I think the story raises questions about the difference between lost love and obsession.

[VII]

The Commandment

I
T WAS EARLY SPRING, 1945. THE RUSSIAN ARMY WAS pressing the Germans near Prague. By train the small farm was three hours from Prague, nestled in a beautiful valley near the Krokonose Mountains. The nearest town, Hostinné, was a two hour walk, and the nearest neighbor a mile distant. Otilie and her husband, Vaclav, and the baby shared a small three-room cabin—two bedrooms and a kitchen. In the kitchen stood a woodstove, a cupboard, a table and two chairs, and a bed for the coldest nights of winter. They believed God had blessed them.

The war had left them unmolested until three months earlier, when Czech resistance recruiters had come for Vaclav. He didn't want to go. They were devout Catholics, she and Vaclav, and they would raise the baby, now six months, in the one true faith. They were also pacifists. They believed, as God had commanded, that "Thou shalt not kill." Vaclav stood by his religious principle, but in the end the recruiters convinced him to go with them to serve as a medic and care for the wounded. Surely God would approve of such a merciful act. So now she was alone with little Bette.

The soldier came at dusk, pushing open the front door of the small cabin, his huge frame almost blocking the evening sunlight from entering the dimly lit kitchen. Their eyes locked, hers wide with fright, his wide with…what? Otilie had never seen a Nazi. Were they all this big, this hardened looking, this ragged and dirty? Was he a brave soldier, separated from his comrades in the fog of battle? Was he a deserter who fled from the onslaught by the Russians? Maybe he is a good man, she hoped, forced by his government to do evil things he regretted. Maybe he has a wife and baby at home, so will show her only kindness and mercy. Such was her prayer.

Without saying a word, he walked to the table, sat down, and ate the piece of bread and moldy cheese she had set out for her dinner. He pointed at the empty plate and said something in German. She spoke no German but understood that he wanted more food. She had very little, had barely survived the winter. It was good that the baby was still suckling.

She gave the Nazi the food from the cupboard. Otilie was glad Vaclav had told her to hide some food under the floorboards. If the Nazi did not kill them, she and the baby would eat again when he left. After eating the food she had put before him, the Nazi laid his head on his crossed arms on the table and simply went to sleep, a dagger in his hand. It was the only weapon she had seen.

She had done as Jesus preached: she had fed the hungry. Surely God would protect her and the baby. She prayed that night, as she did every night, for God to protect Vaclav. That night she prayed for the Nazi's soul, that he be forgiven his sins. She believed with all her heart, because the priest had told her so, that one day she and the Nazis could meet in the Kingdom of Heaven. God had told her that even though she may walk through the valley of the shadow of death, she should not fear evil. That night, she also prayed for God to protect her and the baby from evil, and asked for forgiveness for the fear she *did* feel in her beautiful, peaceful valley that night.

Maybe, she thought, *her prayer would be answered.* Sleep had eluded her, but the Nazi had slept all night at the table and had not hurt them. Could she have wrenched the dagger from his hand as he slept, she wondered? But to what end? "Thou shalt not kill." How many times had God told her that through the night? "Trust in God's will," the priest had always said.

The Nazi awoke with a start, fright in his eyes, raising the dagger as if there were a threat. He saw Otilie and pointed to the empty plate before him. She shook her head and held her hands out to say there was no more food. He stood and looked through the cupboard. No food. Looking around the room, he saw the milk pail by the door. He picked up the pail and walked to where she was seated on the edge of the bed, the baby in her arms crying from hunger. He held out the pail, pointed at her and then at the door, demanding that she get him milk from the cow that must be in the barn. She didn't know how to tell him, so just shook her head no. He slapped her hard, knocking her and Bette back onto the bed, causing the child to cry more loudly. She sat up. He shouted something and again pointed at the pail. She again shook her head no. He backhanded her so hard she thought she might lose consciousness, and the baby wailed in distress. *Jesus, I have turned the other cheek, please protect us*, she prayed.

The Nazi grabbed the pail and left the house. As he approached the barn he detected an odor, and when he opened the door the stench of the long-dead milk cow caused him to retch. He threw down the pail, cursed, and turned back to the house, hungry, angry.

As soon as the Nazi had walked out the door she had offered her breast to the baby. She was sure she would hear him coming back, but she didn't. She looked up to see him standing quietly in the doorway, just as he had the night before. Was it all a dream? She knew it was real when he snatched the baby from her breast and threw it to the end of the bed as if it had been a rag doll. She screamed as he quickly pushed her back onto the bed, straddled her and began sucking the milk from the breast from which he had snatched the baby. She wept and prayed as Jesus had from the cross, *Father, why hast thou forsaken me?* The Nazi began to use his free hand to squeeze her breast hard to get more milk. When no more milk came he sat up, cursed, looked her in the eyes, yet it seemed that he didn't recognize that she, too, had eyes, or a face, or a soul.

Then, in anger and contempt he shouted something strange, "Juden!" He then ripped her dress open, exposing her other breast. He grasped that breast with both hands and squeezed painfully to force out her milk. *No,* she thought, *my baby will starve! Jesus,* she prayed, *I have fed the hungry, even the Devil himself, what more can you ask of me?* She could feel his erection on her leg. He was no longer trying to satisfy just his hunger but was also seeking a different, vile satisfaction.

The Nazi squeezed harder, and her mind registered his use of both hands. She felt on the bed beside her, and grasped the dagger. "Thou shalt not kill" was her thought even as she sliced the dagger across the Nazi's throat. He screamed as blood spurt forth. She pushed with all her strength and they both rolled off the bed onto the floor, she lying on top of him, looking into each other's eyes. His eyes showed surprise, her eyes...what? She felt his arm move and she quickly drove the dagger into his throat until it protruded from the back of his neck. He gurgled, and died. She removed her hand from the dagger. She saw, for the first time, a swastika—a perversion of the cross—on the handle of the dagger. She had killed him. She had defied God, but she was alive, and little Bette would have a life.

Otilie tried to drag the body from the house to bury it in the woods, but it was too heavy. So she buried its pieces in separate small graves scattered throughout the woods. The dagger had been helpful in this. No one would ever know what had happened, what she had done, only she and God. But no, she thought, God would not know, either, because He could not have been there. For the rest of her life she would try to understand why God had forsaken her. Or had He? Was it a test, as God had tested Job? If so, had she failed? Would the Nazi have raped her but not killed her, and is that what God would have preferred? Or was it God who gave her the strength to kill the Nazi? No, that could not be, for it was God who said, "Thou shalt not kill."

Vaclav survived the war, even the Prague Uprising, where he had been those two terrible days when she was fighting her war. He returned unharmed to her and the baby. He had honored God's commandment. He had cared for many wounded, even a few Nazis, but he had killed no one. The resistance fighters who had died in the war were considered martyrs. Those who fought and lived were considered heroes. The priest considered Vaclav to be a special kind of hero because he had found a way to aid the resistance but to also honor God's commandment to not kill. Vaclav gave thanks to

God every day for keeping his family safe while he was away. After the war he attended mass every Sunday until his death, and she was always seated at his side on the pew. Years later, at his funeral mass, the priest praised Vaclav's deep faith and commitment to not kill and extolled his flock always to trust in God. Otilie was uncertain about that. As for her, she would let God do what God would do, but she *was* certain that there are some things a mother must do. After Vaclav's death, she was never seen in church again.

Author's Notes

Perhaps because my father was a veteran of World War II, I often think of Europe through the lens of the war. I have visited the Jewish Museum in Prague, a holocaust memorial. I have been in the tunnels underneath the city that were used by partisans during the Prague Uprising against the Nazis. Bullet damage from that uprising can still be seen on one old building of Charles University.

The inspiration for this story came on a day trip outside Prague to visit a friend. He and his wife and daughter live in a small cabin near a tiny village in the foothills of a beautiful mountain range. On the train I passed through the village of Hostinné. The conflux of the historic sites in Prague, the mountains, and the visit with my friend resulted in this story.

[VIII]
The Gift

HE WAS A FREAK. THAT'S THE WAY PEOPLE LOOKED AT him. That's how he thought of himself. And he *could* think. Bogdan was no Stephen Hawking, but the doctors had told his mother that he had an average IQ, would learn language, but would never be able to speak. His mind was fine, his body useless, muscles contracted into something close to a permanent fetal position, mouth twisted and drawn to one side. He could make sounds, but not words. But he *had* spoken, with his eyes, or some people would say he had.

His father had rejected him, simply leaving after a few years. His mother, surely a saint, had cared for him and his older brother. She told him often that he was a gift from God.

Life for Bogdan was thinking and seeing, seeing limited to what was in front of him and within his peripheral vision as he lay mostly on his left side. He was thankful that he was born in the age of electronics. He liked music, but he loved television. He especially liked the TV preachers.

He was waiting for some TV preacher to explain why a

freak was a gift. The preachers talked a lot about sin and how sinners were punished by God. Had his mother sinned, he wondered? Was he punishment for her sins? But that made no sense to him. Why should he suffer for her sins? Surely no God could be so cruel as to punish one person for the sins of another. Or could He? He had heard a preacher discussing a verse from the Bible about the sins of fathers being visited upon their children. Maybe his birth was punishment for his father's sins, not his mother's; but, no, it was his mother who suffered from his continued life. It must have been her sins.

The preachers told him the Bible is the word of God, and therefore true. Had not God committed the ultimate example of punishing one for the sins of others? Humans had sinned, God was angry, so He killed his own son as punishment for the sins of his other children. He listened to the preachers discuss this story over and over, and he concluded that God is one mean son-of-a-bitch. His mother believed in this God. She prayed to Him regularly. He heard her ask forgiveness for her sins. Perhaps even the sin that gave him to her? Bogdan did not pray. He cursed God every day for the "gift" of his life.

He was about twelve when it happened. It was never

supposed to happen. He wasn't supposed to live that long. Because of his contracted body he could only be bathed while lying in bed. His mother was bathing him as she always did. He felt it begin to swell, could see it grow, and felt an internal pressure that cried out for release. His mother had explained it the first time it happened. It was "normal" she had said. *So, **something** about him was normal*, he thought. It happened a lot. The pressure would build, and then subside slowly. His brother, who was normal (Damn him!) had shown him porn videos (Bless him!). Bogdan knew something about erections and sex.

It was a bath like any other, another erection. His mother rinsed his hair and without looking reached toward the soap at the end of his bed; the soft, soapy, warm, wet skin of the underside of her forearm accidentally sliding across his erection. The pressure from his erection, which previously had always subsided slowly, erupted in a volcanic-like explosion as he grunted and then moaned with an ecstatic release he had never known. The ejaculate was powerful, splattering the length of his mother's arm and striking her in the face. She cursed and recoiled. Immediately she recovered her composure, apologized for her reaction, and assured him that it was "normal."

Even so, he felt a shame he had not known could hurt so badly. His tears flowed, and for the first time his mother heard him speak with his eyes. The two words were clear, as if written, one on each eyeball. *Kill me!* he said. She was visibly shaken. Bogdan blinked, and said it again. She gently rubbed his hair and said, "I love you, son," but her gesture was met with a piercing anger that she had never before seen. She fled the room in tears.

She would never again bathe him. She tried enlisting volunteers, good women from her church, but they could not endure the embarrassment. She hired nannies. They, too, were repelled by his erections and ejaculations, and resigned. She was desperate. He needed a bath. Everyone in Zadar knew about the massage parlors. Some offered only massages. Some offered more. She went to one of the places known to offer "more." She paid for a thirty minute massage. Three places, three massages, three offers to pay to have her son bathed in her home, and three rejections. At the fourth place, a Thai woman agreed to bathe her son for a fee.

Her name was Su Mai, and she was wonderful with him. She simply ignored the ejaculate except to clean it up, and his embarrassment before her soon ebbed. She always smiled at him. He liked her. Eventually, his mother offered to "rescue" Su Mai from the massage parlor, offered her room, board, and a sum equal to what she made at the parlor to be his live-in caretaker. She accepted.

One day when she was bathing him she placed the wash cloth on his erection and he groaned as he always did when it was touched. She looked into his eyes, which she never did when she was bathing him. She saw desire—for relief? For her? She laid the wash cloth aside, continuing to look into his eyes, and took him in her hand and began to gently stroke him. He had never felt anything so good. He came quickly. She smiled. For the first time, she heard him speak with his eyes: *Thank you*. Thereafter, she masturbated him daily during his bath.

It was Christmas, the day the TV preachers and their flocks celebrated the birth of Jesus, God's son, whom He would murder for the sins of others. They exchanged gifts, and he received new videos. Bogdan liked westerns. It was a good day. Su Mai prepared him for his bath, leaned across him, smiled, and grasped his erection. He waited with great anticipation for his relief. Then, with a coy, mischievous smile he had not seen before, she released her grasp. *No*, he thought, *please do it*. She stood and walked around the bed to his blind side. He twisted his eyes as far as he could to the right. She leaned over him, and he could see her head as she lowered it. He felt something soft touch his erection. *Her tongue!* he thought. She kissed the soft tissue of the head of his penis, and then she took it into her mouth. He felt a new level of ecstasy as she moved her head up and down, her lips sliding over that softest of skin. He had seen this in the porn videos his brother had secretly shown him. She was giving him a blow job! He came. In her mouth! He could see her in his peripheral vision as she raised her head, spit into her hand, stood and walked to the bathroom. His heart still racing, his breathing still heavy, she returned to his full vision and said, "Merry Christmas." She saw that his eyes were speaking but she could not hear the words. "I love you," they said.

Their lives continued: he, his mother, Su Mai; the baths,

the masturbation. She had been a part of their family for a year. It was his birthday again, eight more than the ten the doctors had predicted for him. His mother had given him the usual gift, a new video. Su Mai had told him, "I'll give you my gift later." *Another blow job!* he thought, excitedly. She had not done that again since the first time.

He anxiously awaited the evening, his bath, his blow job. She entered his room, stood in front of him, smiled. *Finally!* She began to unbutton her blouse. She had never removed any of her clothing before. *What was she doing*, he wondered? Her blouse fell open, exposing her bra. She looked at him, not smiling, just looking. She removed her blouse, reached behind her, and her bra fell to the floor. He had never seen a woman's breasts. They were small, as she was, and her nipples were dark, almost black. He thought he may be more aroused by the vision before him than he had been from even her touch. *So this was his special birthday gift*, he thought. But then she removed her skirt, revealing small, bright red panties. Could he be more aroused? Yes! She removed the panties, exposing a small patch of dark hair where her legs joined. She cocked one leg outwardly, exposing herself further as her vagina opened slightly, posing for him, still not smiling, just looking into his widened eyes. Then, completely nude, she approached his bed and began removing his clothes. So this was to be his birthday gift, he thought, she would masturbate him in the nude. They were both naked now. He was well-endowed, long, and he believed he had never had a harder erection as he awaited her hand.

She stood in front of him, looked into his eyes, a slight smile on her face now. But she turned away from him; and he then stared at her beautiful ass, wishing, with great frustration, that he could reach out and touch its perfectly symmetrical roundness. *No*, he thought, *don't dress before you touch me!* She didn't. She sat on the bed in front of him; then lay on her side, mimicking his perpetual fetal position. What was she doing? Staring at the back of her head, smelling the cleanness of her long, pitch black hair, he felt her gently grasp his erection and hold it steady as she slowly pushed her body backward, guiding him into her.

He had thought there could be no better feeling than her mouth on him. He was wrong! The most sensitive part of him was surrounded by softness, wetness, warmth. *If the heaven the*

TV preachers talked about is a feeling, this is surely it, he thought. She slowly moved her body back and forth until he exploded inside her. He cried heavily. Yet another level of ecstasy he didn't know existed. She lay there for some time after he ejaculated, he inside her, in absolute silence save for his sobs, until his erection subsided and slid from her. She arose, looked at him with that wry smile, and said, "Happy birthday."

After that day, and for the first time in his life, Bogdan considered that the God the televangelists talked about might be real, and that life may be a gift after all. He now believed that what made his life worth living was daily masturbation, fucking once a week, and a woman he loved; who, surely, must love him. Why else would she do it? But she had never told him that she loved him.

One day she came to him. She had met a man. She had fallen in love. *I thought you loved me,* he thought. *Fuck me now!* his eyes pleaded. She could not, she said. She was sorry he was hurt. She would be leaving soon. There would be someone else to take care of him. She would leave in a month. She would continue the masturbation, she told him, but not the intercourse. He cried that night, all night. The preachers had said that sex for pleasure was a sin. This must be his punishment.

His mother and Su Mai noticed his sudden cough, the difficulty breathing. The doctors could find no cause, but reminded his mother and Su Mai that the length of his life had already been a miracle...a gift. The symptoms worsened over the next days until he would sometimes gasp for breath. It was Su Mai's last week. She bathed him, masturbated him. He coughed and gasped for breath, the same symptoms he had been **feigning** for a month. She told him goodnight and looked into his eyes. His eyes spoke the two words they had once spoken to his mother, *Kill me!* Hearing him, Su Mai was startled, and, frightened, hurried out of the room. She heard him gasping for breath as she fled.

The next night the same routine: bath, masturbation. Then they looked at each other, he again pleading, *Kill me!* He feigned a deep gasp for breath, again pleading with his eyes, *Please, please, kill me!* She looked into his eyes and gave him a kind smile, full of sadness, and pressed the pillow firmly onto his face.

Author's Notes

As a teenager I suffered from low self-image and low self-esteem that resulted in extreme shyness. I often wished I were taller, stronger, smarter, and more handsome. How shallow those thoughts were in the face of so many people in the world suffering from various disabilities and infirmities. As I traveled the world the last few years I have been amazed and humbled at the strength and courage of those damaged, limping, sometimes literally crawling souls on dirty sidewalks; sidewalks that for many are their homes. It is easy to say, "God bless them," but God did not bless them. They need us.

The inspiration for this story came in Zadar, Croatia, an ancient Roman colony. The round column in the heart of the old city forum remains today. When I walked on the stones protruding from beneath the column I was walking on stones tread by Romans 2000 years earlier.

But it was not at that wonderful historic site that inspiration came. It was on a modern, busy street in Zadar that I walked past a man, perhaps in his forties, pushing a wheelchair occupied by a woman about the same age, her body drawn and twisted. His wife? Sister? I will never know, but she was the inspiration for this story.

Three things coalesced to make the story. I thought of a friend who had a son who was severely disabled. Doctors had told her that he would not live past the age of ten. He died when he was thirty. Another friend had told me of working in an institution for the severely mentally disabled, and how the teenage boys would have involuntary erections when she attempted to bathe them. Lastly, I remembered a very good movie, titled *The Sessions*, in which the actress Helen Hunt stars as a professional sex surrogate hired to give a young paralyzed man his first, and possibly only, sexual experience.

[IX]
Vicarious

SHE STOOD BEFORE THE MIRROR NAKED, A SMILE ON HER face as she admired the image she saw: aqua-blue eyes, a perfectly proportioned nose, high cheekbones, full lips, long blonde hair, and firm breasts any woman would envy. She turned slightly to admire the ass that attracted the attention of so many men at work, not over-sized but round and firm and perfect.

Satisfied, Caitlyn dressed for work. The waitresses wore pantyhose (no panties necessary), bright orange shorts, and the tee shirt with the iconic owl, the uniform of the Hooters Restaurant chain. The outfit was designed to tease customers, invite flirtation, and perhaps result in customers ordering more food and drinks than planned. Add a smile and flirtatious conversation, and copious tips were assured.

Inevitably, customers asked the "Hooters girls" out on dates. Although some waitresses were happily married or in stable relationships, most were young, single, free, and open to possibilities. There were few secrets among the girls. When business was slow, they would huddle together and swap stories with low voices and loud laughter. Caitlyn loved it!

⸻

Caitlyn had made him ask several times, only increasing his desire. Finally, she agreed to a weekend at a mountain cabin. He was classically tall, dark, and handsome, with olive skin, pitch black hair, and an Italian accent to boot. The waitresses came to refer to him as the "Italian stallion." His muscles were not large but sculpted, maybe those of a tennis player. He was in America on business for a few weeks.

On the first night at the cabin, he cooked a dinner of pasta with clams and leeks.

"I want to apologize," he called out to her from the kitchen. "The clams are not fresh. I could find only canned. But I made the tagliatelle 'from scratch'—yes?—this is how you say? Just like my mamma taught to me!"

She watched as he deftly crushed garlic cloves with a chef's knife, then cleaned and chopped the leeks and sliced several zucchini, all of which he threw into a pan of sizzling olive oil.

"You should not be afraid of garlic!" he announced with

a smile. "Just make sure everyone has some garlic, then no problem! In Italy, we cannot live without the garlic, but we cannot live also without *amore*," he exclaimed. Caitlyn laughed and assured him that her mouth was watering.

He poured her a tall glass of a crisp white wine that he explained was from the Friuli region of Italy. For dessert he served a molten chocolate cake accompanied with a rich, full-bodied Amaroni. This wine needed to be decanted, he said, but he had forgotten to pack his glass decanter. They searched the cabinets and finally found an old lemonade pitcher. "We will make it work!" he declared, as the velvety wine graced the humble pitcher.

After washing up the dishes together, he produced a small bottle of brandy, which they enjoyed in front of a fire in the cabin's rustic stone fireplace. Drinks led to kissing, and kissing to fondling.

"I want to make love to you," he said.

"No," she said, smiling as he momentarily froze. Then she added, "But you can fuck me."

He picked her up and carried her into the bedroom, tossed her onto the king bed, and began ripping off his clothes. She noticed with some amusement his European-style men's' bikini that did little to hide his bulge. Aroused by his stripping, she, too, removed her clothes. Finally, when she was already naked, he removed his briefs.

"Oh my God!" she inadvertently blurted out. She was staring at the longest, largest penis she had ever seen. He smiled and crawled onto the bed toward her, his erection swaying to-and-fro like a metronome with every advance, his face filled with lust. Kneeling over her and straddling her legs, he stiffened his back, thrusting forward his donkey dick as she now stared with some trepidation.

Then—*somewhat sternly,* she thought—he told her to turn over and get up on her knees. She did. He then mounted her as a jack would mount a jenny. She was relieved when he entered her slowly, with short strokes. But that didn't last. His slow in-and-outs became progressively faster and deeper until she groaned with discomfort. He was too long for her. At least he ejaculated after about fifteen seconds, uttering a sound that she would swear to the girls sounded like braying. He withdrew quickly, grabbing her ass and pushing her to the left as he collapsed, spent, to the right side of the bed.

He kissed her, said, "Thank you," then turned over and fell fast asleep. Beyond the sweet, almost innocent kissing and caressing before they had entered the bedroom, he had shown her no affection, no interest in her needs or feelings. She felt used, and lay awake most of the night feeling angry and sad.

Caitlyn had had enough of the stallion, but there was still another night to go in their "romantic" weekend. The second day, they walked a trail to a mountain overlook with beautiful views where they had a picnic lunch that he had made. It would have been enjoyable if she hadn't spent the whole day dreading the coming night. Most of her thoughts were about how to avoid sex.

All day her conversation was polite but sparse as she attempted to create some distance between them. When they returned from the hike at dusk she quickly showered and dressed in the least appealing attire she had available. They had leftovers for dinner, and again sat before the fire. She refused a second drink, continuing her minimal contribution to the conversation.

Eventually he moved beside her and put his hand on her leg. He leaned in to kiss her, but she moved away.

"Listen," she said. "I'm sorry, but you are so...big...that I'm afraid I'm a little sore."

"Oh, I am sorry," he said, sounding genuinely concerned. "I did not mean to hurt you. You were perfect last night. I could not have been more satisfied. I am sorry it was not the same for you." There was a long silence as they both stared out the window.

He broke the silence, saying, "Caitlyn, I want to make love to you tonight," but she interrupted.

"No, I'm sorry, I just can't."

"No, no, no, please, I'm not talking about intercourse; I just want to make you feel good. Last night I was selfish, but tonight I promise you I can satisfy you completely, with *no* intercourse." She was silent, thinking, and then he began gently stroking the side of her face. She had enjoyed this man's company the first day, finding him kind, courteous, compassionate, and interesting. It was she who had made the second day miserable, at least for herself. She surprised herself when she said, "No intercourse; and just you pleasing me?" "Yes," he replied, "you won't regret it."

She showered after him, while he waited in the living

room, reading. She climbed into the bed, nude but covered by the sheet. Upon hearing her leave the shower, he gave her a few minutes before entering the bedroom. He stood beside the bed, smiled and removed the robe he had worn since his shower. She was encouraged to see that he was wearing, and did not remove, his briefs.

He lay down beside her, and she gave him a reluctant half-smile.

"Please, try to relax. I will keep my promise." He propped his head up with his left hand and reached across her with his right hand, gently stroking her cheek. With light fingertips he caressed her forehead, cheeks and lips before moving down to her neck and the small area of her upper chest that was not covered by the sheet. After hesitating for a moment, he moved the sheet ever-so-slowly downward for an inch before leaning in to make eye contact with her. She turned her head slightly toward him and, eyes locked on each other, gave him a slight smile and nod of her head before breaking eye contact, and returning her eyes to the ceiling before closing them.

After caressing her exposed chest again, he pulled the sheet down just far enough to leave the nipples covered and stroked the exposed tops and cleavage. He detected a slight, subdued gasp as he uncovered the entire breast closest to him. With one finger he circled the breast at its widest diameter, slowly tightening the circle, ever closer to but not touching the nipple. After rising to his knees and doing the same to her left breast, he kissed her chest between the breasts before slowly moving his tongue toward her right breast, circling it with his tongue as he had done with his finger. He blew a breath of warm air onto the hardened nipple before touching it with the tip of his tongue as her back arched reflexively. He pursed his lips around the nipple and sucked softly. She inhaled sharply. He repeated this with her other breast.

Neither of them spoke, and her eyes remained closed. His gentleness had completely relaxed her, put her at ease, and left her quietly hoping for more. She was not disappointed. He pulled the sheet down to the edge of her pubic mound, delicately kissing his way down her stomach, lingering at the belly-button to circle it before gently inserting his tongue. An insertion foretelling the future, she wondered?

Still kneeling beside her, he removed the sheet, revealing her entire nude body, legs closed tightly. To this she opened her eyes and saw his huge erection inside his underwear. Seeing her staring at him, he reassured her. "Don't worry, I promised." He grasped the largest pillow on the bed and asked her to raise her hips, and as she did he placed the pillow under her butt, causing her knees to rise. Still beside her, he started at her neck and, using one finger, circled her nipples and belly-button before dragging the finger across her pubic mound and down the length of her closed legs to her knees.

He moved to kneel at her feet, and, reaching forward, lightly dragged his fingernails from her torso to her knees, raising goose bumps and causing her to shiver. He grasped her feet, slowly separating them as her knees remained together. Reaching around her legs, he again induced a shiver from her as he dragged his nails up the calves of her legs to the underside of her knees. He softly placed his hands on the tops of her knees and began a gentle outward pressure, but her muscles resisted. He stopped and whispered, "It's okay." That was all she needed, and he felt her legs relax.

Continuing the outward pressure with his hands, he slowly opened her, gazing at her shaved body. The night before had been so much about him, he had paid little attention to her;

but now, as he stared down at her, he experienced a thought he had never had before and found himself, without intention, saying softly, "My God, you are beautiful!" He looked up at her face, but her eyes remained closed. Still, he could see her chest rising and falling with quick, deep breaths. On the inner thigh of her right leg, at the knee, he began soft kisses, moving up to the joint of leg and torso, where he licked the soft skin of that joint. He planted one kiss on the left side of her labia, and she gasped in anticipation of what might be next. But it was a tease; and he went to her left leg. This time, after the last kiss, he held his face over her genitals and breathed warm air onto her.

Placing his right hand on her pubic mound, he slowly moved his hand down, softly dragging his middle finger down her vaginal crack, causing her to arch her back slightly. She felt the bed move as he repositioned himself so that he was now prone; and because of the pillow under her butt, her vulva was inches from his face. Beginning at the base of her closed vaginal crack, he slid his tongue to the top, stopping atop her hidden clitoris, pressing against it. He then gently opened her outer lips and licked the incredibly soft skin hidden beneath on both sides; and then the inner lips before slipping his tongue inside her as far as he could. She was very wet and he tasted her slightly salty juices. Her smell was pleasant, fragrant even, but clearly natural. It gave him some kind of animalistic desire to drink of her. It was all he could do to prevent himself from licking and sucking hard, and even biting this thing that could so easily make a frenzied feeding animal of him. But he had promised this gentle woman that he would please her tonight.

Using the thumb and forefinger of his left hand, he spread the vaginal lips to expose her clitoris. He slowly moved his tongue up the left side of her inner lips, pressing against the clitoral hood at the top but going around the little button itself. He circled her clit clockwise several times before circling it counterclockwise, increasing the pace as she responded. After several revolutions he stopped, touched the tip of his tongue to the end of her clitoris and began flicking his tongue up and down, barely touching that extremely sensitive spot. He flicked his tongue up and down and then side-to-side with slightly increased contact. With each new movement he could hear soft gasps; when she would ever-so-slightly press herself toward his mouth he would apply more pressure, or increase the speed of his licking, or simply perform the movement a little longer, giving her whatever she seemed to want.

He stopped licking, and pulling back on the hood to gain maximum exposure of her clit, he pursed his lips, placed his mouth on her and began gently sucking. At this she gasped and then moaned. He alternately sucked and licked as her respiration increased. She had masturbated to a clitoral orgasm, but no man had ever satisfied her, though she had faked a few. While she was in a state of ecstasy the likes of which she had never experienced, she later remembered thinking at this point that there was nothing else he could do to her to bring her to orgasm. She was wrong.

Still alternately sucking and licking her clitoris, he slowly and gently inserted the middle finger of his right hand about two inches into her vagina; and he began making a "come here" movement with the finger causing the finger to press upward against the underside of her clitoris. This resulted in a gasp, a moan, and a slight arch of her back. After less than a minute he removed his finger but quickly replaced it along with his forefinger; but now he pressed both fingers upward and moved them left to right, continuing with his mouth. Again doing something different, he separated his two fingers, pressed upward, and began an in and out motion on either side of her clitoris. Next, yes, there's more! He put the two fingers together again, lowered them and began tapping them up against the underside of her clitoris as he continued to suck and lick her, tap, tap, tap, tap...

Heavy breathing had become gasping and then a cacophony of grunting, whimpering, and *yes* and *ah* when suddenly she began trembling, grasped the bed sheets with both hands, lifted her hips into his face, and began to spasm. She had broken into a light sweat, her head was spinning and her vagina pulsing.

He had stopped sucking and tapping when the orgasm began but kept his fingers inside her now very wet vagina and his mouth covering her clitoris but not moving. When her contractions stopped, he sucked and tapped once and her body convulsed violently. The third time he did that he felt her hand pushing his head away from her. He removed his fingers from her, sat up on his knees between her legs, eyes closed, and began stretching the aching muscles of his neck.

When he opened his eyes she was looking at him, a slight smile with her forefinger at her lips, as if she had been a naughty girl. She looked down at his Spandex bikini, stretched and dark from his ejaculation. He smiled at her and, somewhat embarrassed, said, "Sorry." An involuntary laugh burst from her and she covered her mouth to prevent a further outburst, as if there was something wrong about laughing. But he began laughing, too, and soon both guffawing. He collapsed onto the bed beside her; and she turned to cuddle with him, her head on his chest and leg splayed across him. She said softly, "Thank you." He simply kissed her on the forehead, and they were both fast asleep within minutes.

⁓

He was a handsome, dark-skinned, Arab with coal-black eyes and hair. He was courteous; all the girls liked him. Even fawned over him. They teased him frequently that he must be the rich son of a sheik and took to calling him "the Prince." Finally, he conceded that was true, to an extent. He was a distant relative of the Saudi royal family, and he did have money, lots of it. Caitlyn readily accepted his invitation to fly to Miami for the weekend. He had been a regular customer for months and had readily shown his identification. Besides, all the girls knew their destination, so she felt safe.

The morning flight on the private Leer was fun, as was the day relaxing on the South Shore, with umbrella drinks arriving regularly from the cabana boys of their boutique hotel. They found a Cuban restaurant for dinner; he had curried goat and fried yucca, while Caitlyn did her best to work her way through a delicious but enormous *medianoche* sandwich. He was patient as she shopped the boutiques of Lincoln Road. They walked back to the hotel in the breezy, warm ocean air. He held her hand, which she thought was sweet.

Once at the hotel they changed into comfortable lounge wear. She was standing in front of the window looking out across the ocean when the Prince approached her and put his arms around her waist. She started to turn, but he stopped her. He slid one hand under her shirt, slowly rubbing her tummy, gently inserting a finger into her bellybutton. He whispered softly, "I want you." Silently, she left his embrace, dropped her clothes to the floor, and climbed into bed, pulling the sheet up to her chin. Approaching the bed, he also removed his clothes. He wore "tighty-whities." She suppressed a smile. *Not sexy,* she thought. Even less sexy was what she saw after he took them off. He had the smallest penis she'd ever seen. It was not inordinately short, but its circumference was about the size of her index finger. She had heard the girls talk about this. He had a "pencil dick."

He slid under the sheet next to her. She began to push the sheet down, thinking, actually hoping he would caress, lick, and even nibble her breasts like the Italian Stallion had, now long since returned to Italy. But the Prince whispered, "Turn over, please." She did, and then he pulled the sheet down and completely off her. He began softly caressing her back. He straddled her back and then parted her long hair and tucked it under her shoulders. She thought this seemed odd until he began to caress her shoulders.

Sliding his body down her back, he dragged his now swollen but still tiny penis through the crack of her ass until he was sitting on the backs of her knees. He raised one of his knees so he could press one of her legs outward, repeated the same with her other leg, so that now he was kneeling between her spread legs. She was breathing deeply and nervously. She liked rear-entry vaginal intercourse. But he then spread her cheeks and touched her anus, causing her to clinch her cheeks shut. Before she could say anything, he said, "I want to do it there; it will feel good for me," and then added, "I have a condom."

It wasn't something she had done before, and she didn't like the idea. It seemed gross. But then she remembered his pencil dick. *Jesus*, she thought, *was anal the only way he could orgasm?* She felt sympathy for the Arab, perhaps even a little guilty that he had spent so much money on the trip. She sighed, closed her eyes, and said, "Put the condom on, and be very, very gentle." He promised.

And he *was* gentle, lubricating her generously and entering her slowly. He pushed in and pulled back, the whole time gently caressing her back and butt, constantly repeating an Arabic phrase that of course she did not understand. *Alwald alsaghir aljamil, alwald alsaghir aljamil.* The sex was not very enjoyable for her but not painful either, and, thankfully, she thought, it did not last long. Saying nothing, the Arab curled up to her back, and they both drifted to sleep. They hardly spoke on the flight home the next morning. She explained that she was tired from the wonderful weekend. He didn't return to the restaurant. She never saw him again.

Some months later, Caitlyn was walking downtown running errands on a Saturday. Crossing through the city park, she saw a young woman in a hijab playing with a baby. As Caitlyn smiled and walked past, the woman said, "*Alwald alsaghir aljamil!*" Caitlyn froze. She turned back to the woman. "Excuse me," she said. "I don't mean to intrude, but could you tell me what you just said? I mean, could you translate for me?"

The young woman looked surprised. "This is my son," she said. "I was calling him a 'beautiful little boy.'"

Caitlyn felt a sensation akin to swallowing an icicle. "Oh," she stammered. "Oh, I see. Yes. Yes, he is a beautiful boy." She managed a strained smile. "Thank you," she said, and walked away, staring at, but not seeing, her grocery list.

⌒

Mr. Fancy, as the girls called him, talked a lot about his yacht, not really bragging but expressing genuine pride. He was single, a banker or financier or something, and was always overdressed for Hooters. Even his language was fancy: he spoke very formally, almost like a character from a genteel period movie.

Caitlyn had been on the yacht before, as he had once invited the entire Hooters staff for a holiday party onboard. Now, he had invited Caitlyn and Cindee, a coworker, for a weekend cruise. The day on the boat was wonderful: the moist air cooling their skin in the hot sun, swimming in the cool lake water, floating on rafts, taking full advantage of the yacht's bar and good food, and napping when the sun drained their energy.

There had been no mention of sex in his offer, not even a hint of expectation. Other than respectful compliments about their bikini-clad bodies, the day passed with no sexual insinuations. For all the girls knew, Mr. Fancy was gay. He had been a customer for a year and had never asked any of them out.

The second day, he asked if they would rub on his sunscreen. Cindee replied that she would be happy to, but Mr. Fancy said, "Will you both?" The girls giggled and agreed. He lay on his stomach, and they each applied lotion to their respective sides of his body, then told him to turn over. He did, and an ample erection was standing tall beneath his Speedo swim trunks as if it might burst through the fabric at any moment.

The girls laughed. He apologized, adding that "having you both touch me is extremely stimulating." Neither Caitlyn nor Cindee knew what to say, opting for some noncommittal noises. The subject was dropped.

That evening, their last night on the boat, they recounted the events of the cruise over a candlelit dinner catered by a chef who arrived on a small pontoon boat in the late afternoon, then discreetly packed up and left after the meal. At a pause in the conversation, Mr. Fancy said softly, "It would make this the most perfect weekend I have ever experienced if you would both touch me again."

"It's dark outside, you don't need sunscreen," Caitlyn countered, perhaps a bit curtly. He laughed.

"No, I don't need sunscreen, but I want—I desperately *need* you both to touch me. All of me." Cindee shook her head and matter-of-factly stated, "We are not having sex with you. If you thought that was implied in our acceptance of your invitation you were very wrong."

"No, no, no," he replied, "I'm not suggesting we have sex, not really. I'm just asking you to use your hands. Being with you two beautiful women has created in me a deep need for relief."

"You, my friend, are one smooth bull-shitter," replied Cindee.

"I'm simply suggesting harmless sexual fun," he said. "You owe me nothing for this weekend. Still, I am asking you to do this for me."

No one spoke. Then, Mr. Fancy said, "I'm going to my berth now. I hope beyond hope that you will understand, and that you will knock on my door." He rose and went to his berth.

The girls looked at each other, mouths agape. "Can you believe he asked us to do that?" Caitlyn demanded.

"Have you ever seen such a bull-shitter in your life?!"

They looked across the table at each other, as if taking measure, until Cindee gave a sly smile. Caitlyn started to laugh. "You're not…"

"*You* are!"

"I am *not*! But…"

"You *are* thinking about doing it!"

"Well, like he said, it's harmless, and it's not like you've never jacked off a guy."

"You don't know that."

"Oh, come on."

"Okay, okay, but I've never done it with someone else!"

The girls stared at each other. Then both were on their feet, giggling and racing toward Mr. Fancy's door.

"Oh, please come in!" He was lying on the bed, covered by a satin sheet. Caitlyn, unconsciously—and unnecessarily, since there was no one else on the boat to walk in on them—closed the sliding door behind them.

"There is a God," Mr. Fancy said under his breath, almost prayerfully. The girls smiled but said nothing. They were still wearing their bikinis under sheer cover-ups. Cindee removed her cover-up, and Caitlyn followed suit. They stood there, looking at him. Finally Caitlyn raised both her hands, palms up, to ask, *What now?*

He scooted to the center of the bed. "Please, one of you on each side; begin by caressing my face with your fingertips, working your way slowly down." Cindee kneeled on his left and Caitlyn stepped over him to kneel on his right. The girls began gently touching his face, then, as instructed, slowly worked their way down his body, lingering at his erect nipples, which he asked them to kiss. They did.

His erection had turned the sheet into a tent. The girls paused when they reached his bellybutton.

"Please, don't stop now." The girls lifted the sheet and folded it back to his knees, exposing his impressive erection. They looked at each other, communicating an unspoken, "You go first." Cindee reached out and wrapped her hand around his penis, but he said, "No, fingertips only, please."

They began taking turns wrapping their fingertips about the sensitive underside of his penis and slowly sliding them upward. Caitlyn watched in fascination as his penis changed from pink to light red, dark red, and eventually purple. His breathing became more rapid.

Between panting breaths, he whispered, "Kiss it, please."

"We're not giving you a blowjob," Cindee said.

"Just let me see you touch it with your lips! Please, please," he moaned. Exchanging gazes, each girl, in turn, gently touched her lips, closed-mouthed, to the purple head of his penis. Caitlyn noticed that each time lips touched the soft skin his shaft jerked left.

They went back to the finger-tip caressing, bottom to

helmet. Some seconds ticked by before he spoke again.

"Can I see you kiss each other, please?"

"We're not lesbians," said Caitlyn.

"I know, just please, let me see your lips touch…."

"Say pretty-please."

"Oh, pretty-please."

"Say, I'm begging you."

"I am, **I am**, I'm begging you!"

With him staring in anticipation, they leaned across his body, closed their eyes, and touched their lips together—perhaps for just a little longer than necessary. He moaned.

"Fingers, please," he said, and they returned to their alternate caressing. He was breathing raggedly now, his eyes were flitting back and forth between the two girls. "Oh, who will it be?" he whispered.

Finally, as the girls had begun to worry the purple thing might explode into shrapnel, his penis jerked left and ejaculate spewed out, hitting Cindee squarely in the face. Cindee recoiled and swore like a sailor while Mr. Fancy moaned "Oh, it was you, it was you" and Caitlyn burst into hysterical laughter.

Cindee fled to the bathroom to clean her face. She came back into the room to see Caitlyn pointing at her and laughing so hard she could barely breathe.

Cindee slammed her palm into the wall. "Fuck you!" she yelled at Caitlyn, and then, turning to the limp form of the man, spat out, "Fuck you, too, Mr. Fancy!"

They were all three shocked into momentary silence. The girls had never used that name in front of him.

"Mr. Fancy?" he asked, looking perplexed. Then his expression cleared. "Mr. Fancy!" he exclaimed, beginning to laugh. "Mr. Fancy!"

Caitlyn and Cindee stared at him, then at each other, and then joined Mr. Fancy in speechless, belly-aching laughter.

⌒⌒⌒

Roger had been a regular at Hooters for months. He would speak with the girls cordially when ordering food or drinks, but mostly he would sit alone and do whatever it was he did on his laptop. When Caitlyn asked, he had said he worked in "IT," which gave him the flexibility to work from home or at places like Hooters. Caitlyn noticed that he began to always sit at one of her tables; over time their polite conversations grew longer. Still, two months passed before he asked her out. They went to see a movie, followed by a drink at an up-scale bar. Working in the service industry had made her hyper-aware of how people, especially men, treated others. Roger was polite to everyone and well mannered. Plus, he turned out to be thoughtful and a good conversationalist. Unlike many men she had known, he seemed to understand that the most important part of communication was listening, not speaking. He happily shared his thoughts, but when she spoke she had no doubt that she had his full attention.

Roger was attractive—almost pretty, but not in a feminine sense: he was tall and well-built, with a great head of Robert Redford hair. At the end of their first date she would have welcomed a kiss; instead, he simply gave her a swift kiss on the cheek before stepping away. But he did ask her out again.

For their second date she sat in the stands eating popcorn and watching him play soccer. She had not been thrilled at the prospect when he had asked her to go to the game, but she found herself enjoying it. For one thing, she got to see another side of Roger. As mild-mannered as he was off the field, he was an aggressive player—not an obnoxious jock, but he was clearly invested in the game and rallied his teammates with encouragement, never derision or criticism, and rarely "talked smack" to the other players. After the game they went for ice cream at a sidewalk café and talked and laughed until dark. When he walked her to her door, he again offered a friendly kiss on the cheek, but she caught the side of his head with her hand and steered his mouth toward hers, kissing him. He didn't need any more encouragement. He stepped into her and they wrapped their arms around each other, kissing deeply until he stepped back, took a deep breath, and said, "I should go." His tone conveyed finality, and they both said goodnight. After he'd gone, Caitlyn said aloud to herself, "You could have had me, Roger. Why didn't you take me?"

Their third date was dinner and a play, *Kinky Boots*, a comedy at which they both laughed uproariously. After the curtain closed and they had made their way through coat check and the crowded lobby, he asked if she would like to go to his place for a nightcap; of course she agreed. She was very curious to see where he lived, to get a sense of him through his environment. Plus, she admitted to herself that she wanted to spend as much time with this man as possible. His apartment was immaculate and stylish. She asked him, seriously, if he had employed an interior decorator, but he had not. He put on some easy jazz and went to his bar.

"What can I fix you?" he asked. "I've got all the usual suspects."

"Can you make a Manhattan?"

"Sweet, dry, or perfect?" he asked, to her astonishment. She specified sweet. He made himself a martini, and they sat on the sofa and talked about the play. Eventually, they both sat their glasses on the coffee table. He leaned toward her, and they kissed. After a few minutes, he pulled back his head, looked her in the eyes, and caressed her lips with his finger before coursing it down her neck to her cleavage, which she had exposed via the deep V-neck of her little black dress. He slipped a hand under the dress strap and circled her breast slowly over the lace cup of her black bra. Caitlyn thought she would go out of her mind, *Oh for God's sake, just grab my boob!* she thought. But he didn't. He stopped.

"It's very late, and I should take you home," he said, "but will you promise to have dinner here with me Saturday?"

"I'd love that," she said, and kissed him. "Sealed with a kiss."

She had never anticipated a date like she did this dinner date with Roger. She had never wanted to fuck a man so badly. The week dragged by. When Saturday finally arrived, she drove herself to his apartment. He did not come to pick her up because he was preparing dinner. The man could even cook! Caitlyn had spent the last several days trying to figure out what to wear before giving up and going shopping. She'd bought a new red satin bra to go under a sheer red blouse and a matching thong that wouldn't interfere with the trim lines of her printed cotton skirt.

The dining table was set beautifully, with all the silverware in the right positions (she couldn't help checking, even if at Hooters they simply handed out "roll-ups" of utensils wrapped in paper napkins). Roger had even lit candles. And no, there was nothing she could help him with. He was stuffing whole fresh trout with slices of onion and Meyer lemon. Before sliding them into the oven, he gave them a splash of white wine. Caitlyn looked at the label. "Oh," she said. "I love Friulian wines!"

Roger looked at her with some surprise. "Me, too," he said. "They're different. Like a sauvignon blanc but not as trendy. We'll drink this with the fish. Can I pour you a glass now?"

She accepted, and Roger poured himself some, as well. Roger served the trout with couscous steamed with apricots and Persian spices and chilled, marinated broccolini. For dessert, he proudly announced he had made a molten chocolate cake. Caitlyn almost laughed out loud but managed to keep it to a big smile.

"What?" Roger asked.

"Nothing! I just love molten chocolate cake!"

The meal was delicious. Roger served a ruby port with his molten chocolate cake—"to match your blouse," he said with a wink—which was even better than the Amaroni. This man seemed so unbelievably perfect that she had begun to worry. *Is his imperfection sex? Is that why he has not even tried to have sex with me? Would he tonight?*

They took second glasses of port to the sofa and talked. With him, there never seemed to be an absence of thoughts to share. He arose, turned on some soft jazz with a remote, and held out his hand... "Dance?" She gave him her hand,

and pulling her to him, they moved to the music and kissed. She could feel his erection growing. She was excited yet feared being overly aggressive. After a few moments of dancing, he took a step back and looked into her eyes. She nodded, and, without saying anything, he led her to his bedroom. He began to unbutton her sheer blouse, and she did the same with his shirt. He caressed her breasts as she reached behind herself to unhooked the red bra, letting the straps fall off her shoulders. Roger's hands were on her skin then, his fingers playing lightly over her nipples. Breathing faster now, she reached down and removed his silk boxers, revealing an impressive erection. Receiving this as an invitation, Roger slid her panties down, revealing her smoothly shaved pubis. His eyes widened with a hungry look and she stepped forward out of her thong, gently pushing him back toward the bed. Staring at each other's bodies, they crawled onto the bed. They kissed. He looked into her eyes for a moment and then began circling her nipples with his tongue just as the sultry voice of Nora Jones began singing *Turn Me On*.

"Like a flower, waiting to bloom..." He gently licked and sucked both breasts. *"Like a light bulb, in a dark room..."* He

caressed and kissed her tummy. *"I'm just sitting here, waiting for you…"* He lingered at her bellybutton, circling it and entering it with his tongue while massaging her breasts with one hand as Jones sang, *"to come on home, and turn me on."*

He caressed his way onto her pubic mound where he flattened his hand, placing his middle finger on the vaginal crack between her closed legs. He pressed against her hidden clitoris, with a slow circling motion. After a minute, he pressed his finger down as she opened her legs slightly, allowing him to insert it just inside her vagina. *"I'm just sitting here, waiting for you…"* He could feel her wetness and erect clitoris. *"To come on home and turn me on."*

He returned to face her and she smiled. He began kissing her and returned his hand to her vagina. He massaged her vulva, now moving two fingers in and out while rubbing her clitoris with the palm of his hand.

He raised himself to one knee, placing the other knee between her legs. *"My hi-fi is waiting, for a new tune…"* Looking into her eyes he said, "I want to be inside you." *"My glass is waiting, for some fresh ice cubes…"* Breathing heavily, she simply nodded yes. *"I'm just sitting here, waiting for you…"* He put his other knee between her legs, guided his erection inside her slowly, and lay forward on top of her, returning to kissing her. *"To come on home, and turn me on."*

His movement inside her, to the rhythm of the music, was like nothing she had ever felt before. He did not make deep back-and-forth strokes; but moved in and out only an inch or two. He kept continuous pressure on her clitoris, how, she wasn't sure. Maybe by staying on his toes more than his knees. And he didn't always go straight in and out, but would combine that with a circular motion of his hips. He was massaging her clitoris *while* fucking her. It felt good! She had never had an orgasm from intercourse. She could always feel it building, but there was a wall there she had never climbed. She was climbing it now.

Roger had set the song on repeat. He continued the massaging movements. She could see the tension building in him; feel it nearing the wall in her. They were both panting. The song was just completing its third loop when Roger arched his back, began thrusting, and released a powerful "Ahhhh," still massaging her. His warm ejaculate inside her, her body arched suddenly against Roger, and she came, loudly. They locked their arms around each other, rocking in ecstasy. She had scaled the wall.

When they regained their senses, he rolled over and she laid her head on his chest. They were silent for a few minutes. He broke the silence, "Can I see you tomorrow?"

"Yes."

"Can I see you the next night?"

"Yes."

"Can I see you…"

"Stop it," she chuckled as she cut him off, playfully slapping his chest. After a moment he said, "I think I have to see you every day." She said nothing, but squeezed him tight. *I've found him*, she thought.

⌒

She stood before the mirror naked, tears flowing down her cheeks. She hated the image she saw, her image. Not the beautiful blue eyes of Cindee, but her own plain brown, bloodshot eyes. Not the perfectly sculpted face of Veronica, but her own acne-scarred face with its too-large nose and receding chin. Not the perky set of breasts carried by Jenny, but her own small breasts. Not the sashaying derriere of Lynette, but her own flat butt.

This night she saw her real reflection, not "Caitlyn" but plain Kay. Not the collage of her co-workers that produced the ideal woman her mind usually created in the mirror. Kay was not beautiful, not pretty, never had been. When she was a child, her mother would tell her that she was beautiful, because "every human is a unique creation of God and beautiful in God's eyes." Kay believed that until one night in her early teens, when her mother had tucked her into bed crying from some slight at school. After her mother left, she overheard her father trying to comfort her mother.

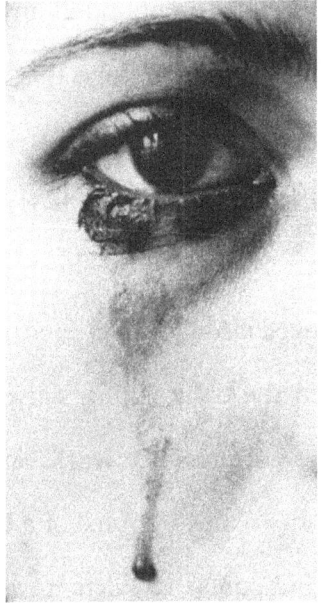

"It saddens me too, but the truth is that our daughter is not beautiful, and all we can do is love her the way she is." Kay waited for her mother's usual admonition, but instead, sounding defeated, she said simply, "I know."

That night ended any hope Kay had ever had of feeling beautiful; any hope that a man, at least one man, might find her attractive for some reason, any reason. She withdrew even further into the lonely shell in which she lived her life.

Now, at thirty-three, she had never had a boyfriend, never even been kissed. She turned away from the painful image in the truth-telling mirror and dried her tears. It was time to get ready for work. She put on her uniform, not the short shorts and tight tee of a Hooters girl, but the plain blue shirt and pants of a kitchen worker who bussed tables and washed dishes. Hopefully, she thought to herself, she would overhear the girls reciting some new sexual adventures into which she could insert herself—or the beautiful collage she imagined herself to be in her nightly fantasies.

Author's Notes

I had thought for a long time about writing a story involving American society's obsession with beautiful women, and of the damage that obsession might do to women who are not beautiful. Billions of dollars are spent on beauty products, clothing, diet plans, and plastic surgery, all in an effort to be beautiful, as defined by society. Many women and, sadly, younger and younger girls struggle with their self-image. In this story, "Caitlyn's" mother is right: every human being is a unique creation and therefore a unique beauty—but how do we make that message believable?

[X]
Doing Good

KEITH DONOVAN JR. AWOKE IN A SWEAT, ABRUPTLY RISING to a sitting position, breathing heavily. The nightmare again. It had been ten years since Nam, but the nightmare took him back there most nights. In fact, he could not remember the last time he slept through the night. She always came to him in his sleep.

He had not been drafted. He had joined, for God's sake, the U.S. fucking Marine Corps, and in 1968! Proof, his fellow jarheads would say, that he was "fucking insane." Not only had Donovan enlisted, he had been in college, so had given up his college deferment. Case closed: "Fucking insane!" That they may be right first occurred to him at Parris Island, a place called a "boot camp" by the Corps and "hell" by the young men who went there to become Marines. *Maybe I am insane*, he thought at the end of his first day on the island. He survived boot camp, then went to Vietnam. One month in-country and he was convinced that his fellow leathernecks were right: he must be fucking insane to have volunteered to go to Nam.

Why had he done it? His father had never talked about serving overseas in the Army during World War II. Was it John Wayne in *The Sands of Iwo Jima* who influenced him? After returning from Nam, he spent the next ten years of his life studying philosophy, obtaining a Ph.D., and seeking an answer to that question.

Donovan was fortunate, returning from Nam to "the world" unscathed but for the nightmare. Many others were not so fortunate. The son of living Marine legend Chesty Puller had followed in his father's footsteps and had gone to Nam as a Marine officer. He had returned home a decorated hero, but had left in the jungle his right leg from the hip down, his left leg below the knee, his left hand, and most of the fingers on his right hand. He struggled like so many injured veterans had, but he became a successful lawyer, not to mention the author of a popular book, *Fortunate Son*, the title drawn, perhaps ironically, from the Creedence Clearwater Revival anti-war song by the same name. Lieutenant Puller had survived Nam and learned to live and be a productive citizen despite his horrible wounds, overcoming great adversity with dignity and courage. Then he killed himself. One more name for The Wall?

He had thought about suicide himself, many times. It was the devastating wounds suffered by Chesty's son and so many others, and those who died in Nam, that kept him alive. His wound, the nightmare, so paled in comparison to their sacrifice that he was shamed into staying alive, or at least into not dying quickly.

After ten years of studying philosophy Donovan concluded that he had joined the Corps and volunteered for Vietnam to do "good" and to fight "evil." He had been raised a Baptist; good and evil were often the themes of sermons. According to the Bible, even God had helped good armies fight evil armies. Everyone agreed that the Nazis and the Japs were the evil armies. In the cowboy movies he loved as a child there were the white hats, the good guys, and the black hats, the bad guys. In Korea, the Godless commies from the north had invaded the peaceful, democracy-loving people of the south. The U.S. government, whom no real patriot believed would lie, had said the same thing was happening in Vietnam: the evil north was attacking the good south. His country called. He volunteered. Simple.

Of course, there had been no mention in high school of the fact that Vietnam had been divided into North and South by the victors of WWII. No discussion of the fact that France had claimed some moral right to make South Vietnam a colony from which it could steal natural riches. No mention of the fact that the French had been defeated in a battle called Dien Bien Phu and had fled the country. No mention of the claim by some that the evil of North Vietnam and the good of South Vietnam were far from clear. All these things he learned studying for his Ph.D. Would the "truth" have changed his mind about volunteering?

One might think that after the incident in the village in Nam, the incident that was the source of his nightmare and the inspiration for ten years of studying philosophy, he would be a pacifist, or at least find peace in religion. Donovan had studied religion extensively, but had concluded that while he believed in God—although he didn't know what that meant—he also believed that the world's religions may bring comfort to their believers but are complete failures at bringing peace to the world. Jesus died, Muhammed lied, Buddha cried, and evil persists. As for "God's chosen people," he concluded that anyone who studied the sad history of those people and chose to be one of them was a foolish martyr.

He had considered pacifism but had concluded that pacifists are either fools or liars, and that pacifism is immoral. Pacifism is an ideal. Donovan had concluded that trying to live an ideal in the real world usually results in tragedy. He considered the case of the professed pacifist who, with his child, is accosted by a man with a gun who threatens to kill the man's child. The pacifist's choice is to fight and, if necessary, kill the attacker, or, on the principle of pacifism, stand by and watch the innocent child, his own child, be murdered. If the man fights and kills the attacker he is a liar, because he is not a pacifist. If he does not fight and allows the attacker to kill his child, he is a fool. He has also committed an *immoral* act of pacifism. To allow a clearly evil person to kill a clearly good person (an innocent child) is, he concluded, unquestionably immoral. If he prayed, he would pray that he would never have to kill again; but the truth is that killing can be necessary, even *good*. That day in the village in Nam the gunny had said, after it happened, "You did good, Marine!" but he saw no good in that day.

Twelve years after Nam he still struggled with the question of who he was. He was a Marine ("Once a Marine always a Marine"), and the nightmare assured he would always live with that. He was no pacifist. He was a patriot: a true patriot, who loved his country but questioned his government and its politicians. Vietnam had taught Donovan that. He was a loner. He had been a professor of philosophy and had enjoyed challenging his young students beyond the bounds of the many filters placed in their minds by their parents, peers, government, schools, and religions. He told them that they were clones of those who put ideas into their minds, and until they critically questioned those ideas and either adopted them as their own or rejected them, they would have no idea who they really were.

His professorship was short-lived. In a discussion on abortion Donovan had suggested, using a legal concept called "party to the crime," that the Pope was a murderer. Consider, he told his students, that two people conspire to commit an armed robbery. One robber enters the store while his conspirator, the getaway driver, waits in the car. The robbery goes bad, and the robber in the store shoots and kills the store clerk. Both the shooter and the getaway driver can be charged with murder, the driver as a party to the crime. The Catholic Church and the Pope proclaim abortion to be murder. At the same time, the Church and the Pope forbid followers from using birth control, which often results in unwanted pregnancies, which in turn may result in abortions. The getaway driver in the robbery did not intend for the clerk to die, and in fact did not see the shooting; however, he was complicit in the murder. The professor concluded that the Pope, who, with the power of his pulpit, denies women the use of protections from pregnancies that often result in abortions, which the Pope considers to be murder, is therefore complicit in those "murders." Was he making a weak analogy, perhaps a false analogy? He didn't care. He had made his students think. He had also made several of his Catholic students very angry. They had complained. The dean had counseled Donovan but had respected his academic free speech.

A few weeks later one of the Catholic students complained again, not about the professor's words this time, but rather about his breath. She reported that he smelled strongly of alcohol in the classroom. Of course he had smelled of alcohol, he drank every day. There was no free speech protection for that offense, and Donovan was fired. For many men his age, being fired, effectively ending a career he actually enjoyed, would be economically, if not psychologically, devastating. But his father, a highly successful Wall Street broker, had died suddenly at age fifty-five. His father had planned well for his family, so neither his mother nor he ever needed to work. His jarhead buddies didn't even know that bit of evidence of his already obvious fucking insanity at dropping out of college, joining the Marines, and volunteering for Vietnam.

A year after being fired from the university, in a bar in Phuket, Thailand, his new "home," Donovan realized he finally had the answer to the question, "Who am I?" He was a drunk, he concluded. He had considered returning to Vietnam; maybe to somehow atone for his sins. Maybe then the nightmare would stop. But in his earlier studies he had concluded that atonement was not possible; a deed done cannot be undone. The nightmare would continue no matter what he did. This was his punishment.

Thailand was close to Vietnam, and very similar. He

once bought an airline ticket to Vietnam but never used it. In Thailand he was the proverbial beach bum. Sun, surf, alcohol, and, oh yes, Thai women. Some were prostitutes, some not. Some would stay with him weeks at a time. He was living what some would consider a dream; he might have thought so himself if not for the nightmare.

His "dream" life in Thailand was simple. Awaken at noon or later, lie under a bamboo shelter on the beach at Phuket, drink until dark, fuck if not too drunk, go to sleep, and wait for the little girl to come in the nightmare. Phuket, Thailand: beautiful beaches, friendly people, and "sex tourism." It had been a favorite R&R destination for American GIs and allied soldiers. The war was history, but wild-west sex still thrived in Phuket. He did not speak Thai, so would invariably find himself in conversations with English speakers at one of his several favorite bars. There was typical bar talk: politics, religion, philosophy, sports, and of course, sex. Sometimes he remembered the conversations (or at least a drunken version of them) sometimes not.

It was a Saturday night like any other. Donovan was drunk, and a Brit struck up a conversation with him. As usual, the talk came around to sex. What was unusual was that the Brit was drunker than he. In their mutual drunkenness they shared funny sex stories. The Brit leaned into him and mumbled, "I'm going for it this time, on Friday."

Donovan asked, also in a drunken mumble, "What, going for what?"

The Brit slurred, "A little girl."

Not sure what he had heard, he asked again, "Going for what?"

The Brit simply said, "What?" as if he didn't remember what had just been said, and the conversation changed.

Later that night, when the Vietnamese girl came to him and he awakened, the Brit's words were in his head: "a little girl." Surely, he thought, the Brit didn't mean a child. Many Thai girls were quite small; that might be what the Brit had meant. Still, Donovan had heard the stories of child sex slavery—children kidnapped or sold by their parents, and then sold for sex with pedophiles. He had never seen any evidence that the stories were true, but he was troubled.

He went back to that bar the next night, and the Brit was there. They drank together, but Donovan drank less than usual. When the Brit was drunk, he asked him, "What did you mean last night when you said you were 'going for a little girl?'" The Brit, though quite drunk, seemed momentarily sobered by the question.

"I don't know what you're talking about." The demeanor of the Brit's denial confirmed for him that he *had* heard the Brit say, "little girl," whatever that meant.

The next night, Monday, Donovan followed the Brit home. On Tuesday he went to the Thai police and told the desk officer the story. The officer listened, uninterested, wrote something, and waved his hand in front of his face, indicating that he smelled alcohol on the complainant's breath. The officer nodded his head and said, "Thank you," in that way that implies, "You can go now." Concerned that the Thai officer didn't take him seriously, he called the U.S. embassy, and was told to call the British embassy. He did. The agent listened to his story, asked a few questions, and said, "Thank you for calling."

On Wednesday night he followed the Brit again, this time to a dimly lit building on a side street. Watching from the shadows, Donovan saw the Brit give money to a Thai man.

Jesus fucking Christ! he thought. This was really happening, and nobody was stopping it.

He lay in bed that night, wondering, in his drunkenness, what he should do. Suddenly he shouted "SMEAC!" The Marine Corps loved acronyms. **S**ituation, **M**ission, **E**xecution, **A**dministration and Logistics, **C**ommand and Signals. "I am," he thought, "a U.S. fucking Marine, and I will not stand by and let a little girl be raped!"

Was he insane? Well, perhaps that question had long-since been settled. But had he misunderstood the situation? Had alcohol permanently damaged his reasoning ability? It didn't matter. He had accepted that he had a mission; he would save the little girl. He reviewed the simple combat order he had written in an effort to focus his drunken mind:

Situation: A little girl was about to be raped.

Mission: Save the girl.

Execution: He would follow the Brit on Friday. If what he feared was true, if a little girl was going to be raped, he would intervene and use whatever force necessary to rescue the girl.

Aministrtion and Logistics: He knew that intervening in something like this could result in violence. He had hoped that he would never have to kill again after Vietnam, but he accepted the real world. He bought a K-bar, the famous Marine combat knife, and a red-lensed military flashlight from a pawn shop.

Command and Signals: He was alone. There was nobody to communicate with.

The success of military missions depends on good intelligence. On Thursday night Donovan had gone back to the building where the Brit had paid the Thai. He observed that the area was poorly lighted and that one Thai man stood outside the front door. He found a damaged back door and gained entry into a hallway with four doors. Using his dim, red-lensed combat flashlight he looked into three of the rooms. They were empty. In the fourth room, the closest to the front door, there was a lamp and a mattress on the floor. "Damn!" he said aloud, "This must be where it will happen." There was a doorway in the room that led to the side of the building. The door was missing but the opening had been covered with boards. He used the K-bar to pry enough of the bottom boards loose for him to make a crouching entry into the room from outside if necessary. There were small gaps between the boards, wide enough that he should be able to see into the room if the lamp were on. "Of course it will be on," he muttered, "the sick bastard wants to see her."

His reconnaissance had provided the details of the execution of his mission. If all went well Donovan would burst through the loosened boards, grab the girl, and rush back through the hole in the doorway before the Brit or the Thai at the front door could react. His mission was a classic combat raid. Success depended on surprise and speed.

He wondered whether this mission was insane. But he concluded that if he did not accomplish the mission, a little girl's life would be ruined or even lost. The girl's value to the traffickers would be diminished once she was no longer a virgin. Would the traffickers kill her? He questioned his ability to accomplish the mission. He had not been drunk since Saturday night—well, only half drunk—but he was what people called a functional alcoholic. He put aside his doubts. "I'll do good tomorrow, Gunny," he said to himself.

He didn't know what time Friday the Brit was supposed to be at the building, so he decided to sleep outside the Brit's house Thursday night and follow him all day. As always, the nightmare came that night. It was always the same. The platoon, two squads on line and one in reserve, was ordered to occupy a village thought to be harboring Viet Cong. His platoon was in a rice paddy, behind the berms, the village in view. The lieutenant gave the signal to move out. It was quiet, low voices on the radios between the lieutenant and the squad leaders, the sucking and sloshing sound of boots in the paddies, the heat punishing.

Closer now, but still quiet; then a shot, a scream, a Marine went down, someone shouting "Corpsman, Corpsman!" Someone else shouted, "The hooch on the left flank!" The lieutenant yelled, "Return fire!" All hell broke loose. Everybody, including him, unleashed American firepower onto a tiny straw hut. The M-16s repeated short popping bursts while the M-60 machine guns, the "hogs," cranked out their mellow sound of sustained rapid fire until

the lieutenant gave the signal to cease fire. The seconds of madness ended, and relative quiet returned.

The hut was mangled but could still provide concealment, if the sniper was alive. His squad was the closest to the hut. Donovan and a buddy were ordered to move forward and clear the hut while the rest of the platoon stood ready to provide covering fire if needed. They approached slowly, cautiously, weapons at the ready. He tore the hanging straw door from the hut, and he rolled in left while his buddy rolled right. They scanned their sectors of the hooch with their eyes and their weapons. The enemy soldier, the sniper, was on the floor, weapon beside him, multiple gunshot wounds in his body, obviously dead.

In the light streaming through the damaged hut they saw the others, an old man and woman, perhaps in their seventies, their bodies bloody and riddled with bullet holes, their eyes open with the death stare. A younger man, maybe the son of the old couple, was lying on top of a woman about the same age. Trying to protect her perhaps? Four dead civilians, what the military called "collateral damage." He had seen it before. An unfortunate hazard of war, his leaders had said; the dead were likely enemy sympathizers, they had said. Possibly that was true. It was better to believe that it was.

His buddy turned to exit the hut and give the all-clear, but Donovan yelled, "Wait!" He had seen feet protruding from a bamboo mattress at the rear of the hut. He took the five steps forward to reach the mattress, weapon at the ready, buddy backing him up. He reached down, grabbed the mattress and threw it aside, his weapon pointed center mass of the threat. The threat was a six-year-old little girl. He knew it was a girl because she was naked. Donovan couldn't tell by her face, because she had no face. Where her face had been was a bloody mess of white tissue, bone, and brain matter. Her face had been shot away. His buddy just said, "Damn!" But Donovan lowered his weapon, stared, until he felt the bile rising from his stomach, and ran from the hut, dropping to his knees, dry heaves at first and then puking up what felt like six months of C-rations. He puked until every muscle in his body ached. The gunny saw him, walked over, put a hand on his shoulder and said, "You did good today, Marine."

The nightmare of the faceless little girl, and the drinking, began that night and had not stopped. She was persistent. VA counseling had not kept her away; nor had VA drugs. Drinking helped keep her away when he was awake, but nothing kept her from coming in his sleep.

He followed the Brit all day Friday; evening brought them to their usual bar. The Brit waved when he entered the bar but did not invite him to sit at his table as before. The Brit drank lightly and walked out of the bar early. He followed the Brit to the building, watched him talk to the Thai at the front door, and then enter. He hurried to his hiding place on the side of the building and peered into the room through the cracks in the loosened boards. The small, dim light was on. The Brit was lying on the mattress, naked. He almost gave his position away when he gasped upon seeing a naked little girl, this one with a face, a frightened face.

The Brit motioned for the girl to come to him. She shook her head, no. "Come!" the Brit yelled angrily, and she obeyed. The Brit was sitting up, holding the girl with one hand, touching her with the other, breathing heavily, no, panting, like an animal. The Brit suddenly lay back, pulling the girl forward so that she was astride his stomach; and then, putting his hands under her arms, raised the little girl up, grasped his erection with one hand and began pushing the girl down with the other.

This was it! Donovan burst through the loosened boards on the doorway. The little girl screamed, broke away from the Brit's grasp and ran to a corner of the room, where she cowered. The Brit turned away from him, reaching for something. A handgun! There was no choice. Holding the Brit's head down with one hand, he slit his throat with the K-bar, blood gushing from an artery. The door opened. There had been another Thai guard in the hallway! He lunged forward from a crouching position and gutted the man. He heard a voice down the hall—the Thai from the front door? Donovan closed the door and waited, back against the wall. The door opened slowly. An arm with a gun in hand broke the plane. He came down as hard as he could with the K-bar, almost severing the hand. The Thai screamed and he pushed the K-bar up, underneath the ribs and into the heart. Three dead, and all in seconds. *I did good, Gunny*, he thought. He went to the girl, still huddled in the corner. He tried, unsuccessfully, to calm her. Then he picked her up into his arms and ran from the building. He would go to the police and tell his story.

What the people in the street saw was a blood-splattered

Anglo carrying a naked, crying little Thai girl. As taunts from bystanders and followers grew louder he walked faster, then ran. He was caught, the girl snatched from his arms, and he was beaten by the crowd until police arrived; then he was beaten by the police. He thought he would die. The little girl saved him, finally convincing the police that he had saved her from others. The police took him back to the building and surveyed the bloody scene. He was arrested and jailed.

A few days later, a Diplomatic Security Agent from the U.S. Embassy in Bangkok visited him. The agent was seated at a table in the jail visitation room, a manila folder on the table. Donovan sat down across from the agent. The agent said, "You fucked up, jarhead."

He stared at the agent. Only another Marine can call a Marine "jarhead" without offense.

"One-nine, Nam." Marine lingo for 1st Battalion, Ninth Marine Regiment, 2nd Marine Division, Vietnam veteran.

"Two-one, Nam."

"I know," the agent said. "I read your jacket."

Having established that they were brother Marines, he

asked the agent, "When do I get out of here?" The agent looked at him with what may have been a combination of sympathy and confusion. "What do you think is going to happen here?"

"I guess I'll stay here until the investigation is complete, and when it's clear that I rescued a six-year-old girl from being raped I'll be released. I'm not in the Corps, so they can't give me a medal, I guess."

"You're fucking insane," said the agent.

Here we go again, he thought. The agent continued, "You killed three people, a British national and two Thai nationals. You're being charged with three counts of murder."

"Murder? That wasn't murder! I killed those men in self-defense while on a mission to rescue an innocent child from rape, and possibly murder. That's not murder, and that's not insane. Allowing that to happen would have been insane."

"You were on a 'mission'?" the agent asked. "You're a fucking civilian in a foreign country; you didn't have a *mission*! You should have let the authorities handle this."

"I tried!" he shouted, barely controlling his anger. "I called the U.S. Embassy, and you did nothing."

"We have no authority over a British national; and you

were advised to contact the British Embassy."

"I did! They said they couldn't act on a first name, an address, and drunken murmurs that I wasn't sure I heard correctly."

"Then you should have contacted the Thai police."

"I *did*, goddamn it!" he shouted, "The cop basically ignored me, but he did write something down."

The agent pursed his lips, shook his head slowly, and said, "The Thai police say they have no record of ever talking with you. The Thai government says that stories of child sex slavery in Thailand are lies."

At trial, most communication was through a translator, but the judge had apparently learned a little English for the occasion. The judge said, "U.S.A. law no allow vigilante. Thailand law no allow vigilante." Before announcing sentence, the judge asked him if he wanted to make a statement. He quoted Edmund Burke, "All that is needed for evil to triumph is for good men to do nothing." Unimpressed, the judge sentenced him to life in prison.

Donovan was quietly doing his time, hoping for the best. The DSS agent had told him the U.S. would seek a reduction in his sentence through diplomatic channels. He was sober. The nightmare still woke him every night, but now when he threw the bamboo blanket off the naked little Vietnamese girl in the hut, she had a face, the smiling face the little Thai girl had the last time he saw her in court. Was that atonement? He didn't believe in atonement.

Only ten months had passed when he heard the jailhouse rumor. The guards, who seemed sympathetic, had treated him well but would not confirm the rumor. He asked to see the Diplomatic Security Service agent. When he asked the agent if it was true, the agent looked away and said, "You shouldn't have asked me to come here."

"All I want is the truth, brother."

"Yes," the agent replied, "the girl's addict mother sold her." The agent paused. "Again."

"Again? You mean…?"

"Yes."

He sat there, staring at nothing, tears streaming down his face. The agent excused himself and vowed to return the next day.

That night, when in the nightmare he threw aside the

bamboo mat, he awoke with a start, having seen again the bloody mess of the faceless Vietnamese girl. He lay awake, his mind a jumble of nonsensical thoughts. "SERE!" he shouted. Another Marine Corps acronym: **S**urvival, **E**vasion, **R**esistance, **ESCAPE**!

I am, a U.S. fucking Marine, he thought. *And I will not stand by and let a little girl be raped!*

Author's Notes

The inspiration for this story arose in Ho Chi Minh City (previously Saigon), Vietnam, in 2011. I was sitting in a nice restaurant on the Saigon River. Across the river the land was undeveloped and there were rice paddies for several hundred yards back from the river to a tree line. Just inside the trees could be seen several straw huts. As my mind wandered I began to think about how I would assault that village. I am *not* a Vietnam veteran; but I am a veteran and a Marine, at least in the "once and always" sense. I was not sent to Vietnam because of my entry into active duty near the end of Marine Corps combat operations there, but I had trained to go there and had "assaulted" a mock Vietnamese village that may have looked like the one I saw from the restaurant.

I began to form a story about assaulting a village, but I wanted to write something about the emotional scars some warriors bring home from their wars; thus, the nightmare of the faceless girl. At first I was going to have our protagonist return to Vietnam, but then I remembered seeing a news show discussing sex slavery, particularly child sex slavery in Thailand. Perhaps this story will shine some light on this evil reality that some find difficult to discuss.

Acknowledgements

Even though they would likely not approve of this book, I must give thanks to Momma and Daddy for always encouraging me to think for myself.

This book would never have been completed without the advice, counsel, expertise, and friendship of my editor, Lee Ann Pingel of Expert Eye Editing. Her editing of both grammar and content made my stories better, and for that I shall forever be grateful.

Lee Ann would like to thank Richard Shoemaker of Athens, GA, who, by sharing a similar story of his own, helped solve the problem of getting the young protagonist of "Forgiveness" into a position where he could see the nun (artistic license has been taken).

Thank you also to Bowen Craig and William Bray of Bilbo Books Publishing, and to their graphic designer, Dan Roth of Athens Creative Design.

About the Author

Allen Woods resides in Providence, RI. He retired after thirty-three years working in the criminal justice system, and has taught college-level criminal justice courses. He can be contacted through his publisher.

www.ingramcontent.com/pod-product-compliance
Lightning Source LLC
Chambersburg PA
CBHW060450280326
41933CB00014B/2715